The Observation Guide

Working with Young Children

by
Dr. Judy Herr
Professor, Early Childhood Education
College of Human Development
University of Wisconsin–Stout
Menomonie, Wisconsin

Publisher
The Goodheart-Willcox Company, Inc.
Tinley Park, Illinois

Contents

Part 2
Creating a Safe and Healthy Environment

Part 3
Guiding Children

Part 4
Learning Experiences for Children

Part 5
Other People You Will Meet

Introduction

The *Observation Guide* is designed for use in early childhood education classes. Its chapters are coordinated for use with the text *Working with Young Children,* although it can be used in any early childhood education program. This product gives you the opportunity to carefully observe and learn from a variety of children and child care settings.

The *Observation Guide* provides forms and instructions so that you can gain the most from your observations of children and early childhood programs. It is divided into chapters that coordinate with the chapters of *Working with Young Children.* Early observations are designed to help you become familiar with observation and recording techniques. As the chapters progress, your involvement in observations will become more advanced. In later chapters, you will plan, lead, and evaluate your own activities.

Each observation experience begins with objectives for the activity. Instructions for any preparation needed are given. Space to record information on the setting and activities of the observation are given as well. Questions are also provided to help you summarize and interpret your observations.

This observation guide should be used to supplement learning from textbook reading and classroom lecture. You should have a good basic understanding of the subject matter before conducting each activity. Then you can use the guide to apply what you have learned to real classroom situations.

Why Observe Children?

Young children are fascinating to watch. Just ask any new mother, father, or proud grandparent! A young child's awkward attempts to try new skills or early efforts at conversation can be captivating. Observing children is something everyone enjoys doing.

Observation also serves another purpose. It is one of the oldest methods of conducting research. Most of what is known about child growth and development is the result of some form of observation. Many behaviors of children cannot be measured in any other way. For instance, a one-year-old can't answer questions verbally or in writing, but the child's behavior can be observed.

Data gathered from formal observation has been used to establish developmental norms. These norms include physical, cognitive, social, and emotional aspects of development. They include characteristics considered normal for children in specific age groups. These norms assist teachers in comparing and noting changes in the growth and development of young children in their care. They will also help you as you observe young children in preparation for your career in child care.

Forms of Observation

Early researchers recorded the behavior of each child in a diary. They attempted to record every important event that occurred. This was very time-consuming. Researchers later developed a variety of forms that made observations simpler and more precise. Three types of forms that are used in this guide are narrative, checklists, and rating scales. The type of form used depends upon what is being observed.

Narrative

The simplest form of observation is called *narrative.* The child's behavior is described in detail as it occurs. This is the first of two processes involved when using the narrative form of observation. Only this process is completed during the actual observation time. The second process, called *interpreting,* occurs after the observation takes place.

When you use the narrative form of observation, your eyes will be acting like a camera. You will be recording pictures of children playing, learning, and interacting. During your observation, you will record how children communicate, both verbally and nonverbally. You will record how they look and what they do. You'll note physical gestures and movements. You will also detail children's interactions with people and materials.

During the observing process, it is important to record only objective statements. To be objective, a statement must pass two tests. First, it must describe only observable actions. Generalizations about the motives, attitudes, and feelings of the children are not included. Secondly, the recorded information must be nonevaluative. It should not include why something happened, nor imply that what happened was wrong, right, good, or bad. Labeling should be avoided. No judgments or conclusions should be inferred at this point. The following is an example of a narrative observation:

Sally arrived at school holding her mother's hand. She slowly walked over to her locker, removed her coat, and hung it in her locker. She turned to her mother and said, "You go to work." Sally's mother hugged her and said, "After work I'll take you to the dentist." Sally looked up at her mother and started to cry. She said, "I'm not going to the dentist. I'm staying at school." Sally's mother reached out and hugged Sally. Sally continued crying and hung onto her mother. The teacher walked over to Sally and whispered in her ear. Then the teacher put out her hand and said, "Come and look, Sally. We have a new friend at school today. Jodi brought her new hamster." Sally stopped crying and took the teacher's hand. Together they walked over to see the hamster. Sally's mother watched her for a moment and then left the room.

Notice that only an objective description of the observed behavior is recorded. The statements do not include any of the following: causes, desires, emotions, explanations, goals, motives, or needs.

To help you learn to write an objective narrative, complete the following exercise. Then turn to page 10 for the answers.

Self-Test

Read each statement. Place a *D* in front of those statements that are descriptive. Place an *I* in front of those statements that are interpretive.

_____ 1. Jose opened the door and ran outside.

_____ 2. Mark left the block building area because he wasn't interested.

_____ 3. Mrs. Devery, the teacher, called each child's name.

_____ 4. When the bunny was taken out of the box, the children were so excited that they screamed.

_____ 5. The teacher's aide said, "I like how quietly you are sitting."

_____ 6. The volunteer asked each child to name one color.

_____ 7. May cried because she could not speak English.

_____ 8. Kris hit Kelsi because she was in his way.

_____ 9. Wendy tipped over her glass of milk.

_____ 10. Maurice put the rabbit in the cage, shut the door, and closed the lock.

_____ 11. Tuanda walked across the room and sat next to Judy.

_____ 12. Sandy was confused by the teacher's directions so she took another cookie.

Once the narrative data is recorded, a second process begins. This process involves interpretation of the data. An attempt is made to explain the observed behavior and to give it meaning. Why did the child behave as he or she did? What might have been the child's motives? Did someone or something cause the child to act in this way? This interpretation takes knowledge and skill. It should not be attempted without a thorough understanding of how children grow and develop. The observation itself serves no purpose without this interpretation of behavior to give meaning to the data.

Though an observation may be factual and unbiased, various interpretations are sometimes made. Since no two people are exactly alike, no two people will interpret facts in the exact same way. Each person who interprets a child's behavior may determine different motives for the behavior based on their own personal experiences. Their personal feelings, values, and attitudes may also influence the interpretation of behavior.

To illustrate, an observer wrote the following:

Tony picked up the pitcher of milk. He moved the pitcher toward his glass. He hit the glass and tipped it over. The milk spilled.

In reviewing the observation of Tony, his behavior might be interpreted in several ways:
- Tony was careless.
- Tony was inexperienced in handling a pitcher.
- Tony wasn't paying attention to what he was doing.
- Tony lacked the strength needed to lift the pitcher.
- Tony lacked the hand-eye coordination necessary to pour from the pitcher.

To decide which interpretation is most accurate, you would need to observe Tony on several occasions over time. You would also need a thorough understanding of how children grow and develop.

Checklists

Another form of observation is the *checklist*. Checklists are easy to use. They include specific behaviors to look for while observing a child or group of children. The targeted behaviors are listed in a logical order. You can quickly record the presence or absence of a behavior.

Rating Scales

Rating scales are used to record the degree to which a quality or trait is present. Where a checklist only indicates the presence or absence of a trait, a rating scale tells how much or how little is present.

Rating scales are easy to do and require little time to complete. Some rating scales contain only a numerical range. Others define the behaviors more specifically. In order to decide on a rating, the observer should have a good understanding of the behaviors he or she is rating.

Preparing to Observe

When you are assigned an observation activity from this guide, you should first read through the entire form. Study the objectives to determine the purpose for the observation. Then note the specific behaviors you will be looking for or the events you will be recording. It is important to know ahead of time what you will be focusing on during the observation.

After determining the purpose for the observation, you will need to decide where you will observe. You may need to make arrangements to visit a child care facility. Select an appropriate location and call for an appointment. Ask to speak to the director. Explain the purpose of your visit. Decide on a time that is mutually convenient and will not interfere with normal operations at the child care facility. If you are unable to be at the facility at the scheduled time, call the center and reschedule the observation. For some activities, your instructor may make arrangements for the entire class to observe at the same time. If your school has its own child care laboratory, outside arrangements will not always be necessary. Your teacher will schedule your observation time.

Each of the observation forms in this guide follows a similar format. Record all the information requested, such as the name, address, and telephone number of the facility you are visiting. Indicate the name and title of the contact person. On most of the forms, you will be asked to record the names and ages of the children you observe.

The date and time of the observation should also be noted. Record the time when you begin your observation. After you finish, record the exact time the observation ended. This is important information. The time of day can be a factor when interpreting a child's behavior.

Guidelines for Observers

During your study of young children, you will observe them in many situations. When on the play yard, in a classroom, or on a field trip, your behavior is important. Whether you are in an outside child care facility or in your school's own laboratory, certain guidelines must be followed.

Whenever you gather data about children, you must use special care. The information you collect must be kept confidential. This is perhaps the most important guideline for you to follow. Though you can discuss a child's behavior in your own classroom, you must refrain from doing so outside of that setting. Whenever you are talking, other people are listening. The information you share could be embarrassing or even damaging to a child, parent, or teacher.

To protect confidentiality, your teacher may request that you avoid using a child's name during classroom discussions. First names only are permitted in other classrooms. Both practices will help protect the real identity of a child. These practices will also prevent information about a particular child from leaving the classroom.

When you arrive at the center, check in with your contact person. If you are visiting a large school or center, you may be asked to sign a visitors' log. This is a record of all the people who are visiting the school. You may be asked to record the time you arrive, person you are visiting, purpose of your visit, and the time you leave.

If this is your first visit to a center or school, you may have to ask some questions. Always ask where to place your personal belongings. Coats, books, and other personal belongings should not be brought into the classroom. Young children are especially curious about purses and bags. Such items may cause an unnecessary distraction. Cosmetics and medications could endanger their safety.

As you enter the classroom, you will need to communicate with the teacher in charge. However, be sensitive to what is happening in the room. Enter the room quietly so that you do not disrupt the activity. If the teacher is working with a group of children, avoid interrupting. Find a place to sit or stand and wait for the teacher to approach you. If the children are involved in a self-selected play period, pause by the door until the teacher acknowledges your presence.

Introduce yourself to the teacher. If he/she is not involved and time permits, share your observation sheet. Indicate the length of time you will be present. Ask the teacher where he or she would like you to be while you observe the children. This will typically be a place where the children will not be distracted by your presence.

During your observation time, avoid talking to the children, other observers, or the staff. However, it is likely that your presence will spark the curiosity of some of the children. A child may ask you what you are doing. If this happens, answer in a matter-of-fact manner. You might say that you are watching the children play or that you are writing notes on how children play.

At the end of the observation period, leave the room as quietly as possible. If the teacher is not involved with a group of children, extend your appreciation. Otherwise, a nice gesture is to leave a thank-you note. You might place it on the teacher's desk or leave it with a secretary, director, or principal. You could also mail or e-mail the note.

While at an observation site, always remember that you are a guest at the center or school. If you behave improperly, you may be denied future observation privileges. Your behavior at the observation site will reflect on your school or department. Improper behavior could prevent other students from observing at the site.

Answers for the Self-Test on Page 8

1. Objective. Describes an observable behavior.
2. Interpretive. "Because he wasn't interested" refers to an inferred motive.
3. Objective. Describes observable behavior.
4. Interpretive. "Were so excited" is an inferred motive for screaming.
5. Objective. Describes observable behavior.
6. Objective. Describes observable behavior.
7. Interpretive. "Because she could not speak English" is an inferred motive for crying.
8. Interpretive. "Because she was in his way" is an inferred motive for hitting.
9. Objective. Describes observable behavior.
10. Objective. Describes observable behavior.
11. Objective. Describes observable behavior.
12. Interpretive. "Was confused by the directions" is the inferred motive for taking another cookie.

You: Working with Young Children

Teacher Responsibilities

Activity A

Chapter 1

Name _____

Date _____ **Period** _____

■ Objectives

After completing this activity, you will be able to
■ identify responsibilities of an individual in the child care profession.
■ discuss how responsibilities may vary depending upon the position.

■ Preparation

1. Make arrangements to spend a minimum of one hour with a nanny, au pair, kindergarten teacher, child care teacher, child care director, preschool teacher, or licensing specialist.
2. Study the types of responsibilities outlined in the text for the position chosen.

■ Setting

Place _____

Address _____

Telephone number _____

Contact person_____ Title _____

Name of person observed _____

Individual's position _____

Date _____ Time _____ to _____

Number of children present (if applicable)_____

Ages of children (if applicable) _____

Other information _____

_____

_____

■ To Do

Observe a child care professional for a minimum of one hour. Record his or her responsibilities and the time spent on each.

(continued)

Name_____

Time	Responsibilities

_____

_____

_____

_____

_____

_____

_____

_____

_____

_____

_____

_____

_____

_____

_____

_____

_____

_____

_____

_____

■ To Review

1. What responsibilities seemed to take the most time?

_____

_____

_____

_____

_____

2. How might the individual's responsibilities vary depending upon the time of day?

_____

_____

_____

_____

Types of Early Childhood Programs

Selecting Child Care

Activity A	**Name** _____
Chapter 2	**Date** _____ **Period** _____

■ Objectives

After completing this activity, you will be able to
■ evaluate an early childhood program.
■ identify your own feelings about the child care program.

■ Preparation

1. Make an appointment with a child care director to discuss his or her program and observe the facility.
2. Review the questions on the chart below.

■ Setting

Place _____

Address _____

Telephone number _____

Director's background:
  Name _____

  Education _____

  Teaching experience _____

  Length of time working in center _____

Date _____ Time _____ to _____

Size of staff _____ Number of programs _____

Number of children enrolled_____

Other information _____

■ To Do

As you talk with the director and tour the center, complete the chart below. Then answer the questions that follow.

	Yes	No
Do the children appear to be happy, active, and secure?		
Are staff meetings conducted regularly to plan and evaluate program activities?		
Are all staff members trained in early childhood education?		

(continued)

	Yes	No
Do staff attend in-service training and professional meetings and conferences on a regular basis?		
Do staff observe, assess, and record each child's developmental progress?		
Does the curriculum support the children's individual rates of development?		
Is the indoor and outdoor environment large enough to support a variety of activities?		
Is the environment inviting, warm, and stimulating?		
Is equipment provided to meet all four areas of development—social, emotional, cognitive, and physical?		
Are safe and sanitary conditions maintained within the building and play yard?		
Are teacher-child interactions positive?		
Are teachers using developmentally appropriate teaching strategies?		
Are parents welcome to observe and participate?		
Is there sufficient equipment for the number of children attending?		
Does the climate in the center "feel" positive?		
Is the center accredited by the National Academy of Early Childhood Programs?		
Do teachers meet with parents regularly to discuss the child's needs, interests, and abilities?		

What three questions indicate the program's greatest strengths?

_____

_____

_____

What three questions indicate the program's greatest weaknesses?

_____

_____

_____

As a parent, would you send your child to this center? Why?

_____

_____

_____

_____

As a teacher, would you want to work at this center? Why?

_____

_____

_____

_____

Observing Children: A Tool for Assessment

Writing Anecdotal Records

Activity A

Chapter 3

Name_____

Date_____ **Period**_____

■ Objectives

After completing this activity, you will be able to
■ write an anecdotal record.
■ evaluate an anecdotal record for its objectivity.

■ Preparation

1. Arrange to observe a child in a preschool, child care center, or Head Start center.
2. Review the content of an anecdotal record listed below.

■ Setting

Place _____

Address _____

Telephone number_____

Contact person_____ Title _____

Date _____ Time _____ to _____

Child's name _____ Age_____

Other information _____

_____

_____

■ To Do

Review the contents of an anecdotal record listed below. Observe a child and record an incident on the form provided. Finally, evaluate your anecdotal record.

Contents of anecdotal records

- identify the child and the child's age
- include the setting
- identify the observer
- provide an accurate account of the child's actions and conversations
- include responses of other children and/or adults involved in the situation

(continued)

Anecdotal Record

Child's Name: _____ Date: _____

Child's Age: Years: _____ Months: _____

Setting: _____ Time: _____

Observer:_____

Incident: _____

_____

_____

_____

_____

_____

_____

_____

_____

_____

■ To Review

1. Review your anecdotal record. Does it include who was involved, what happened, when it happened, and where it occurred? Explain.

_____

_____

_____

_____

_____

_____

2. Did your record include how the children communicated verbally and nonverbally? Explain.

_____

_____

_____

_____

(continued)

3. Was all the recorded information observable? Explain.

_____

_____

_____

_____

_____

4. Was the recorded information nonevaluative? Explain.

_____

_____

_____

_____

_____

5. Was an objective description of the observed behavior recorded? Did your statements include emotions, motives, desires, needs, or wishes? Explain.

_____

_____

_____

_____

_____

6. Why is it important to keep your observations objective?

_____

_____

_____

_____

_____

Using a Checklist

Activity B

Chapter 3

Name _____

Date _____ Period _____

■ Objectives

After completing this activity, you will be able to
■ use a checklist to record the presence or absence of specific traits or behaviors.
■ evaluate the use of checklists.

■ Preparation

1. Arrange to observe a three- or four-year-old child in a preschool, child care, or Head Start setting.
2. Review the skills list in the checklist.

■ Setting

Place _____

Address _____

Telephone number _____

Contact person _____ Title _____

Date _____ Time _____ to _____

Child's name _____ Age _____

Other information _____

_____

_____

■ To Do

As you observe the child, put a check in the column marked *yes* if you observe the behavior. If the child is unable to perform the behavior, check *no*. If the behavior is not observed, do not check either column.

	Gross Motor Skills	**Yes**	**No**
	Walks on tiptoes.		
	Performs a standing broad jump for 8½ inches.		
	Attempts to balance on one foot.		
30 to 36 months	Walks to and picks up large ball.		
	Balances on one foot for five seconds.		
	Catches a large ball with arm.		
	Walks up stairs with alternating feet.		
	Rides a tricycle.		
	Performs one to three hops with feet together.		

(continued)

	Gross Motor Skills	Yes	No
37 to 48 months	Walks toe-to-heel for four steps.		
	Balances on one foot for eight seconds.		
	Catches a beanbag while standing.		
	Performs one to three hops on one foot.		
	Catches a bounced ball with hands.		
4 years	Hops on one foot.		
	Walks down stairs with alternating feet.		
	Throws a ball overhand.		
	Carries cup of liquid without spilling.		
	Rides bicycle with training wheels.		
	Balances on one foot for ten seconds.		
	Skips with alternating feet.		
	Walks backwards toe-to-heel for four consecutive steps.		

■ To Review

1. Contrast the use of this checklist with the writing of an anecdotal record.

   _____

   _____

   _____

2. What advantages and disadvantages do you see in the use of a checklist?

   _____

   _____

   _____

   _____

3. Describe a situation where you would use a checklist as a form of assessment and explain why.

   _____

   _____

   _____

   _____

   _____

(continued)

4. Describe a situation where you would *not* use a checklist for assessment and explain why.

_____

_____

_____

_____

_____

Activity Preferences During Self-Selected Play

Activity C

Chapter 3

Name _____

Date _____ Period _____

■ Objectives

After completing this activity, you will be able to
- ■ use a participation chart to assess activity preferences during self-selected play.
- ■ evaluate children's activity preferences during self-selected play.

■ Preparation

1. Arrange to observe a small group of children in a preschool, child care center, or Head Start center.
2. Review the codes for individual activities listed under the chart.
3. Record the hour you will observe under the time column.

■ Setting

Place _____

Address _____

Telephone number _____

Contact person _____ Title _____

Date _____ Time _____ to _____

Other information _____

_____

_____

Child's Name	Age

(continued)

Name_____

■ To Do

Write the names of the children in the spaces provided. Insert the hour of your observation in the left-hand column. Review the codes listed under the chart. For each 10-minute segment, record the activity or activities in which each child participated. For example, if a child only played with manipulatives for the first 10-minute segment, record an *m* in the space provided. If the child moved from block building to storytelling during that time period, both a *b* and *st* need to be recorded in the space.

Activity Preferences During Self-Selected Play						
Children's Names						
__:00 - __:10						
__:10 - __:20						
__:20 - __:30						
__:30 - __:40						
__:40 - __:50						
__:50 - __:00						

a=art; b=blockbuilding; dp=dramatic play; m=manipulative; s=sensory; sc=science; st=storytelling

■ To Review

1. Which child remained engaged in one activity for the longest period of time? Explain.

_____

_____

_____

_____

_____

_____

2. Which child moved most frequently from activity to activity? Explain.

_____

_____

_____

_____

3. Which activities did the children engage in the most? Explain.

_____

_____

_____

_____

(continued)

Name_____

4. Which activities did the children engage in the least? Explain.

_____

_____

_____

_____

5. How could you use the information gained from this assessment tool?

_____

_____

_____

_____

Rating Scale

Name _____

Date _____ Period _____

■ Objectives

After completing this activity, you will be able to
- ■ use a rating scale to record the degree to which a quality or trait is present.
- ■ evaluate the use of rating scales.

■ Preparation

1. Arrange to observe a three-year-old child in a preschool, child care, or Head Start setting.
2. Review the skills list on the checklist.

■ Setting

Place _____

Address _____

Telephone number_____

Contact person_____ Title _____

Date _____ Time _____ to _____

Child's name _____ Age_____

Other information _____

_____

_____

■ To Do

As you observe the child, rate each category of social play as *always, usually, sometimes,* or *never.*

Social Development	Rating			
	Always	**Usually**	**Sometimes**	**Never**
Spends time watching others play				
Plays with toys alone				
Plays with toys similar to others'				
Makes contact and plays with other children				
Likes to be accepted by others				
Gives and takes while interacting with peers				
Gains access to engaging with others in a positive manner				

(continued)

Name_____

Social Development	Rating			
	Always	Usually	Sometimes	Never
Interacts in harmony with peers				
Sees things from another child's point of view				
Shares possessions and toys with peers				
Respects others' rights				
Strives for independence				
Expresses anger verbally rather than physically				
Resolves play conflicts in a positive manner				

■ To Review

1. What are the advantages and disadvantages you see in the use of rating scales?

_____

_____

_____

_____

_____

2. Describe a situation where you would use a rating scale for assessment and explain why.

_____

_____

_____

_____

3. Describe a situation when you would *not* use a rating scale as a form of assessment and explain why.

_____

_____

_____

_____

Understanding Children from Birth to Age Two

Observing Motor Development

Activity A

Chapter 4

Name _____

Date _____ Period _____

■ Objectives

After completing this activity, you will be able to
- ■ define *motor development*.
- ■ identify motor skills of children from birth to age two.
- ■ report specific information about the observation setting.
- ■ describe methods teachers use to support motor development.
- ■ list classroom equipment that promotes motor development.

■ Preparation

1. Arrange to observe an infant and a toddler. (More than one visit may be needed to complete the activity.)
2. Review the motor skills listed on the charts on the following pages.

■ Setting

Place _____

Address _____

Telephone number _____

Contact person_____ Title _____

Date(s) _____ Time(s) _____ to _____

_____ _____ _____

_____ _____ _____

_____ _____ _____

Infant's name_____ Age_____

Toddler's name _____ Age_____

Other information _____

_____

_____

■ To Do

As you observe each child, mark the column next to each motor skill the child has mastered with the month and date the skill was observed. If you wait a few months between observations, you will observe each child's progress.

(continued)

	Motor Skills	Date Observed
1 Month	Does not control body movements since movements are still reflexive.	
	Needs support for head. Without support, head will flop backward and forward.	
	Lifts head briefly from the surface in order to turn head from side to side when lying on tummy.	
	Twitches whole body when crying.	
	Keeps hands fisted or slightly open.	
	May hold object if placed in hand, but drops it quickly.	
	Follows moving object briefly if the object is within the line of vision.	
2 Months	Can keep head in midposition of body when lying on tummy.	
	Can hold head up for a few minutes.	
	Can turn head when lying on back.	
	Cycles arms and legs smoothly. Movements are mainly reflexive, but may begin to become voluntary.	
	Grasps objects in reflex movements, but grasps are becoming voluntary.	
	May hold object longer, but drops object after a few minutes.	
	Uses improved vision to look at objects more closely and for a longer time.	
3 Months	Can move arms and legs together.	
	Turns head vigorously.	
	Can lift head for several minutes.	
	Can sit briefly with support.	
4 Months	On tummy, can lift head and chest from surface, using arms for support.	
	On tummy, may roll from side to side.	
	Can maintain a sitting position for several minutes if given proper support.	
	Uses hands more skillfully.	
	Begins to use mitten grasp for grabbing objects.	
	Looks from object to hands to object.	
	Swipes at objects, gradually improving aim.	

(continued)

Name_____

	Motor Skills	Date Observed
5 Months	On back, can lift head and shoulders off surface.	
	Can roll from tummy to back.	
	When supported under arms, stands and moves body up and down, stamping feet alternately.	
	Helps when being pulled to a sitting position.	
	Can sit supported for 15 to 30 minutes with a firm back.	
	Reaches for objects such as an activity gym with good coordination and aim.	
	Begins to grasp objects with thumb and fingers.	
	Grabs objects with either hand.	
	Transfers objects from one hand to the other, dropping objects often.	
	Can hold a cube in hand.	
6 Months	Rolls from back to tummy.	
	On tummy, moves by pushing with legs and reaching with arms.	
	Gets up on hands and knees, but then may fall forward.	
	Is able to stand while supported.	
	May be able to sit for short periods of time.	
	Reaches with one arm and grasps object with hand, then transfers the object to other hand. Reaches for another object.	
	Holds an object in both hands.	
	Learns to drop an object at will.	
	Sits in a tripod position using arms for support.	
7 Months	Crawls awkwardly, combining movements on tummy and knees.	
	Likes to bounce when in standing position.	
	May be able to pull self to a standing position.	
	Can lean over and reach while in sitting position.	
	Has mastered grasping by using thumb in opposition to fingers.	
	Holds an object in each hand. Brings objects together with banging noises.	
	Keeps objects in hands most of the time.	
	Fingers, manipulates, and rattles objects repeatedly.	

(continued)

	Motor Skills	Date Observed
8 Months	Sits alone steadily for longer periods of time.	
	Crawls.	
	Achieves sitting position by pushing up with arms.	
	Learns pincer grasp, using just the thumb and forefinger.	
	Is able to pick up small objects and string.	
9 Months	Sits alone.	
	May try to crawl up stairs.	
	May be able to move along furniture, touching it for support.	
	Uses index finger to point, lead, and poke.	
10 Months	Likes to walk holding on to caregiver's hands.	
	Climbs on chairs and other furniture.	
	Stands with little support.	
	Can release grasped object instead of dropping it.	
11 Months	Stands alone.	
	Is able to stand and pick up objects.	
	Likes to grasp feeding utensils and cup.	
	May carry spoon to mouth in feeding attempt.	
	Takes off shoes and socks.	
12 Months	Climbs up and down stairs.	
	May show preference for one hand.	
	May be able to take off clothes.	
	Walks with one hand held.	
13 to 15 Months	Builds a tower consisting of two one-inch cubes.	
	Turns pages in a book two or three at a time.	
	Walks without assistance.	
	While walking, cannot maneuver around corners or stop suddenly.	
	Scribbles vigorously.	

(continued)

Motor Skills		Date Observed
16 to 18 Months	Walks up steps.	
	Walks well while carrying a toy or pulling a pull toy.	
	Hurls a ball.	
	Can place six round pegs in pegboard.	
19 to 22 Months	Completes a three-piece formboard.	
	Places four rings on post in random order.	
	Rolls, pounds, squeezes, and pulls clay.	
	Kicks backward and forward.	
	Walks up stairs independently, one at a time.	
	Jumps in place.	
22 to 24 Months	Attempts to stand on balance beam.	
	Builds tower of six cubes.	
	Runs without falling.	
	Pedals a tricycle.	
	Kicks a large ball.	

■ To Review

1. Define *motor development.*

_____

_____

_____

_____

_____

2. In your observations, what did the teachers do to advance the development of motor skills?

_____

_____

_____

_____

_____

_____

3. List equipment you observed in the classroom that is designed to promote the development of motor skills.

_____

_____

_____

_____

_____

_____

Observing Cognitive Development

Activity B

Chapter 4

Name _____

Date _____ Period _____

■ Objectives

After completing this activity, you will be able to
- ■ define *cognitive development.*
- ■ identify cognitive skills of children from birth to two years of age.
- ■ report specific information about the observation setting.
- ■ describe methods teachers use to support cognitive skills.
- ■ list classroom equipment that promotes cognitive development.

■ Preparation

1. Arrange to observe an infant and a toddler. (More than one visit may be needed to complete the activity.)
2. Review the cognitive skills listed on the chart beginning on this page.

■ Setting

Place _____

Address _____

Telephone number _____

Contact person_____ Title _____

Date(s) _____ Time(s) _____ to _____

_____ _____ _____

_____ _____ _____

_____ _____ _____

Infant's name_____ Age_____

Toddler's name _____ Age_____

Other information _____

_____

_____

■ To Do

As you observe each child, mark the column next to each cognitive skill that the child has mastered with the month and day the skill was observed. If you wait a few months between observations, you will observe each child's progress.

	Cognitive Skills	Date Observed
1 Month	Prefers to look at human faces and patterned objects.	
	Listens attentively to sounds and voices.	
	Cries deliberately for assistance; also communicates with grunts and facial expressions.	
	Is comforted by human voices and music.	

(continued)

	Cognitive Skills	Date Observed
2 Months	Coordinates eye movements.	
	Shows obvious preference for faces to objects.	**10 to 12 Months**
	Makes some sounds, but most vocalizing is still crying.	
	Shows some interest in sounds and will stop sucking to listen.	
3 Months	Is able to suck and look at the same time, thus doing two controlled actions at once.	
	Discovers hands and feet as an extension of self.	
	Searches with eyes for sounds.	
	Begins cooing one-syllable, vowel-like sounds—*ooh, ah, aw*.	
	Laughs out loud.	
4 Months	Likes to repeat enjoyable acts such as shaking a rattle.	
	Enjoys watching hands and feet.	
	Looks at an object, reaches for it, and makes contact with it.	
	Makes first consonant sounds—*p, b, m, l*.	
	Smiles and coos when caregiver talks to him or her.	
	Explores toys by grasping, sucking, shaking, and banging.	
5 Months	Recognizes and responds to own name.	
	Smiles at self in mirror.	
	Can recognize people by their voices.	
	Babbles spontaneously.	
6 Months	Grabs at any and all objects in reach.	
	Studies objects intently, turning them to see all sides.	
	Varies volume, pitch, and rate while babbling.	
	Acquires sounds of native language in babbles.	
7 Months	Anticipates events.	
	Produces gestures to communicate; points to desired object.	
	Enjoys looking through books with familiar pictures.	
	May begin to imitate an act.	
	May say *mama* or *dada* but does not connect words with parents.	

(continued)

	Cognitive Skills	Date Observed
8 Months	Likes to empty and fill containers.	
	Begins putting together a long series of syllables.	
	May label object in imitation of its sounds, such as *choo-choo* for train.	
	Finds objects that are totally hidden.	
9 Months	Responds appropriately to a few specific words.	
	Likes to look for contents in a container.	
10 to 12 Months	Waves good-bye.	
	Speaks first recognizable word.	
	Links specific acts or events to other events.	
	Can point to body parts.	
	Likes to look at pictures in a book.	
	Puts nesting toys together correctly.	
	Begins to find familiar objects that are not in view but have permanent locations (looks for cookies after being told he or she can have one).	
13 to 15 Months	Identifies family members in photographs.	
	Gives mechanical toy to caregiver to activate.	
	Has an expressive vocabulary of four to ten words; most nouns in vocabulary refer to animals, food, and toys.	
16 to 18 Months	Demonstrates knowledge of absence of familiar person (points to door, says "gone").	
	Enjoys cause-effect relationships (banging on drum, splashing water, turning on the television).	
	Has expressive vocabulary of 10 to 20 words.	
19 to 24 Months	Mimics adult behaviors.	
	Points to and names objects in a book.	
	Has expressive vocabulary of 20 to 50 words.	
	Sorts shapes and colors.	
	Refers to self by name. Recognizes self in photo or mirror.	

(continued)

■ To Review

1. Define *cognitive development.*

_____

_____

_____

_____

_____

2. In your observations, what methods did the teachers use to promote the development of cognitive skills?

_____

_____

_____

_____

_____

3. List equipment you observed in the classroom that promotes the development of cognitive skills.

_____

_____

_____

_____

_____

Observing Social-Emotional Skills

Activity C

Chapter 4

Name _____

Date _____ Period _____

■ Objectives

After completing this activity, you will be able to
- ■ define *social-emotional development.*
- ■ identify social-emotional skills of children from birth to two years of age.
- ■ report specific information about the observation setting.
- ■ describe methods teachers use to support social-emotional development.
- ■ list the classroom equipment that promotes social-emotional development.

■ Preparation

1. Arrange to observe an infant and a toddler. (More than one visit may be needed to complete the activity.)
2. Review the social-emotional skills on the charts beginning on this page.

■ Setting

Place _____

Address _____

Telephone number _____

Contact person_____ Title _____

Date(s) _____ Time(s) _____ to _____

_____ _____ _____

_____ _____ _____

_____ _____ _____

Infant's name_____ Age_____

Toddler's name _____ Age_____

Other information _____

_____

_____

■ To Do

As you observe each child, mark the column next to each social-emotional skill that the child has mastered with the month and day the skill was observed. If you wait a few months between observations, you will observe each child's progress.

Social-Emotional Skills		Date Observed
1 Month	Reacts to discomfort and pain by crying for assistance.	
	Makes eye contact.	
	Is comforted by the human face.	

(continued)

	Social-Emotional Skills	Date Observed
2 Months	Is able to show distress, excitement, contentment, and delight.	
	Can quiet self by sucking.	
	Looks at a person alertly and directly. Prefers to look at people over objects.	
	Quiets in response to being held.	
	Shows affection by looking at person while kicking, waving arms, and smiling.	
3 Months	Shows feelings of security when held or talked to.	
	Senses that the hands and feet are extensions of self.	
	Whimpers when hungry; chortles when content.	
	Communicates using different sounds and facial expressions.	
	Responds with total body to a familiar face.	
	Tries to attract attention of caregiver.	
	Watches adults' facial expressions closely.	
4 Months	Expresses delight and laughs.	
	May form an attachment to one special object.	
	Responds to continued warmth and affection.	
	Shows increased pleasure in social interactions.	
	Enjoys social aspects of feeding time.	
	Becomes unresponsive if left alone most of waking hours.	
5 Months	May begin to show fearful behavior as separateness is felt.	
	Distinguishes between familiar and unfamiliar adults.	
	Builds trust when cries are answered; becomes anxious and demanding when cries are unanswered.	
	May be able to play the "peek-a-boo" game.	
6 Months	Enjoys playing with children.	
	Responds to affection and may imitate signs of affection.	
	Likes attention and may cry to get it.	
	May begin clinging to a primary caregiver.	
	Laughs when socializing.	
	Smiles at familiar faces and stares solemnly at strangers.	

(continued)

	Social-Emotional Skills	Date Observed
7 Months	May show more dependence on caregiver for security.	
	Has increased drive for independence but senses frightening situations.	
	Shows desire for social contacts.	
	Thoroughly enjoys company of siblings.	
	Begins to have a sense of humor.	
	Expresses anger more dramatically.	
8 Months	Exhibits fear of strangers.	
	May anticipate being left and, if so, becomes disturbed.	
	Values quick display of love and support from caregiver.	
	Likes to explore new places, but wants to be able to return to caregiver.	
	Enjoys playing with own image in a mirror.	
	Definitely prefers caregiver to strangers.	
	Is more aware of social approval or disapproval.	
9 Months	May show fear of heights; may be afraid to crawl down from a chair.	
	May show a fear of new sounds.	
	Shows interest in play activities of others.	
	Likes to play games such as pat-a-cake.	
	Recognizes the social nature of mealtimes.	
	Performs for an audience, repeats if applauded.	
10 Months	Cries less often.	
	Expresses delight, happiness, sadness, discomfort, and anger.	
	May be able to show symbolic thought by giving love to a stuffed toy.	
	Is more aware of and sensitive toward other children.	
	Enjoys music and may mimic movements others make to music.	
	Fears strange places.	
11 Months	May not always want to be cooperative.	
	Recognizes the difference between being good and being naughty.	

(continued)

	Social-Emotional Skills	Date Observed
11 Months (cont.)	Seeks approval and tries to avoid disapproval.	
	Imitates movements of other adults and children.	
	Likes to say "no" and shake head to get response from a caregiver.	
	Tests caregivers to determine limits.	
	Objects to having his or her enjoyable play stopped.	
12 Months	May reveal an inner determination to walk.	
	Begins to develop self-identity and independence.	
	Shows increased negativism. May have tantrums.	
	Enjoys playing with siblings.	
	Likes to practice communication with adults.	
	Continues to test caregivers' limits.	
	May resist napping.	
13 to 15 Months	Shows pride in personal accomplishments.	
	Likes to exhibit affection to humans and to objects.	
	Prefers to keep caregiver in sight while exploring environment.	
	Demands personal attention.	
	May show fear of strangers.	
	Shows increased negativism. Becomes frustrated easily.	
	Enjoys solitary play.	
	Shows preference for family members over others.	
16 to 18 Months	Is emotionally unpredictable and may respond differently at different times.	
	Is unable to tolerate frustration.	
	May reveal negativism and stubbornness.	
	May exhibit fear of thunder, lightning, large animals, and strange situations.	
	Is very socially responsive to parents and caregivers.	
	Responds to simple requests.	
	May punch and poke peers as if they were objects.	
	Is unable to share.	

(continued)

Social-Emotional Skills		Date Observed
19 to 21 Months	May become possessive about toys, hiding them from others.	
	Likes to claim things as "mine."	
	Gives up items that belong to others upon request.	
	Begins to show empathy to another child or adult.	
	Continues to desire personal attention.	
	Indicates awareness of a person's absence by saying "bye-bye."	
	May enjoy removing clothing and is not embarrassed about being naked.	
	Reveals a sense of trust in adults.	
	Plays contentedly alone if near adults.	
	Likes to play next to other children, but does not interact with them.	
	Is able to play some simple interacting games for short periods of time.	
22 to 24 Months	Displays signs of love for parents and other favorite people.	
	Is easily hurt by criticism.	
	Shows the emotions of pride and embarrassment.	
	May show some aggressive tendencies, such as slapping, biting, and hitting.	
	May assume an increasingly self-sufficient attitude.	
	Wants own way in everything.	
	May dawdle but desires to please adults.	
	Is more responsive to and demanding of adults.	
	Still prefers to play alone, but likes to be near others.	
	Engages in imaginative play related to parents' actions.	
	Uses own name in reference to self when talking to others.	
	Is continually testing limits set by parents and caregivers.	
	Likes to control others and give them orders.	

(continued)

■ To Review

1. Define *social-emotional development.*

_____

_____

_____

_____

2. In your observations, what methods did the teachers use to promote the development of social-emotional skills?

_____

_____

_____

_____

_____

_____

3. List equipment you observed in the classroom that promotes the development of social-emotional skills.

_____

_____

_____

_____

_____

_____

Understanding Two- and Three-Year-Olds

Observing Two- and Three-Year-Olds

Activity A

Chapter 5

Name _____

Date _____ Period _____

■ Objectives

After completing this activity, you will be able to
- observe the appearance of a two-year-old and/or a three-year-old.
- observe the child's development.
- describe the types of activities in which the child needed adult assistance.

■ Preparation

1. Make arrangements to observe a two-year-old and/or a three-year-old child in a child care or preschool program.
2. Review the developmental characteristics of a child this age described in the textbook.

■ Setting

Place _____

Address _____

Telephone number _____

Contact person_____Title_____

Date _____Time _____to _____

Child's name _____ Birthdate _____

Age_____ Height _____ Weight _____

Other information _____

■ To Do

Respond to the items listed below during your observation of the child.

Physical Development

1. Describe the child's physical appearance.

_____

_____

_____

_____

(continued)

2. How do the child's height and weight compare with other children the same age?

_____

_____

_____

_____

_____

Motor Skills

3. Describe the child's fine motor and gross motor skills.

_____

_____

_____

_____

_____

4. Compare the child's motor skills with those expected at this age. (Refer to the textbook if needed.)

_____

_____

_____

_____

_____

Cognitive Development

5. What evidence of the child's thinking processes have you observed?

_____

_____

_____

_____

Language Development

6. Describe the child's language skills.

_____

_____

_____

_____

_____

(continued)

Social-Emotional Development

7. Describe the child's social and emotional development.

_____

_____

_____

_____

_____

8. How does the child compare with the other children in the same age group?

_____

_____

_____

_____

_____

_____

Self-Help Skills

9. Describe the self-help skills this child was able to do. Provide specific examples.

_____

_____

_____

_____

General Characteristics

10. Describe the child's behavior. Note whether it was typical or atypical of children this age.

_____

_____

_____

_____

_____

_____

_____

Development of Two- and Three-Year-Olds

Activity B

Chapter 5

Name _____

Date _____ Period _____

■ Objectives

After completing this activity, you will be able to
■ observe general characteristics of two-year-old and/or three-year-old children.
■ recall the children's physical, social, emotional, and cognitive development.
■ describe the types of activities the children seem to enjoy.
■ describe the relationships of the children with one another and with adults.

■ Preparation

1. Make arrangements to observe a group of two-year-olds and/or three-year-olds in a child care, preschool, or Head Start program.
2. Review the developmental characteristics given in the textbook.

■ Setting

Place _____

Address _____

Telephone number _____

Contact person _____ Title _____

Date _____ Time _____ to _____

Number of children _____ Number of adults _____

Other information _____

_____

_____

■ To Do

Observe the group of children for at least one hour. Then answer the questions below.

1. Describe incidents or examples of general characteristics of two-year-olds and/or three-year-olds listed in the text that you observed.

_____

_____

_____

_____

_____

_____

_____

_____

_____

_____

(continued)

Name_____

2. List the physical skills and motor behaviors the children demonstrated.

_____

_____

_____

_____

_____

_____

_____

_____

_____

_____

3. Describe the relationships of the children with the adults and with one another.

_____

_____

_____

_____

_____

_____

_____

_____

_____

4. Describe the types of activities the children appeared to enjoy.

_____

_____

_____

_____

_____

_____

_____

_____

_____

_____

50

Observing Developmental Characteristics of Two-Year-Olds

Activity C

Chapter 5

Name _____

Date _____ Period _____

■ Objectives

After completing this activity, you will be able to
- ■ identify gross motor, fine motor, self-help, social, emotional, math readiness, and language skills of a two-year-old child.
- ■ report specific information about the observation setting.

■ Preparation

1. Make arrangements to observe a two-year-old child. (More than one visit may be needed to complete the activity.)
2. Review the skills on the charts on the next pages.

■ Setting

Place _____

Address _____

Telephone number _____

Contact person _____ Title _____

Date(s) _____ Time(s) _____ to _____

_____ _____ _____

_____ _____ _____

_____ _____ _____

Child's name _____ Age _____

Description of observational setting _____

_____

_____

_____

Other information _____

_____

_____

■ To Do

As you observe the child, mark the column next to each skill that the child has mastered with the month and day the skill was observed. If you wait a few months between observations, you will observe the child's progress.

(continued)

Gross Motor Skills		Date Observed
24 to 29 Months	Runs without falling.	
	Begins to use pedals on a tricycle.	
	Kicks a large ball.	
	Jumps in place.	
	Plays on swings, ladders, and other playground equipment with fair amount of ease.	
	Throws ball without falling.	
	Bends at waist to pick up object from floor.	
	Walks up and down stairs, both feet on step, while holding on to railings.	
	Stands with both feet on balance beam.	
30 to 36 Months	Walks on tiptoes.	
	Performs a standing broad jump 8½ inches.	
	Attempts to balance on one foot.	
	Walks to and picks up a large ball.	
	Balances on one foot for five seconds.	
	Uses arms to catch a large ball.	
	Walks up stairs with alternating feet.	
	Rides a tricycle with ease.	
	Performs one to three hops with both feet together.	
Fine Motor Skills		
24 to 29 Months	Inserts key into locks.	
	Turns pages in a book one at a time.	
	Strings large beads.	
	Copies a vertical line.	
	Copies a horizontal line.	
	Builds a tower consisting of six to seven cubes.	
	Uses two or more cubes to make a train.	
	Uses one hand consistently for most activities.	

(continued)

Observing Developmental Characteristics of Two-Year-Olds (Cont.)

Name_____

Fine Motor Skills		Date Observed
24 to 29 Months (cont.)	Holds scissors correctly.	
	Opens and closes scissors.	
30 to 36 Months	Builds a tower consisting of eight cubes.	
	Copies an *H.*	
	Copies a *V.*	
	Copies a circle.	
	Imitates building a three-block bridge.	
	Snips paper with scissors.	
Self-Help Skills		
24 to 29 Months	Cooperates in dressing.	
	Removes shoes, socks, and pants.	
	Pulls on simple garments.	
	Unzips zipper.	
	Unsnaps snap.	
	Verbalizes toilet needs.	
	Usually remains dry during the day.	
30 to 36 Months	Seldom has bowel accidents.	
	Unbuttons large buttons.	
	Closes snaps.	
	Sits on toilet without assistance.	
	Puts on shoes.	
	Pours well from a pitcher.	
	Uses a knife for spreading.	
Expressive Language Skills		
24 to 29 Months	Combines two or more words. "Boy hit."	
	Developing three-term relations such as "I kick ball," "You go home," "See my daddy."	
	Yes/no questions marked only by intonation. "Mommy go?" "You see me?"	
	No and *not* used to negate entire sentence. "No eat." "Mommy no." "No sit down."	

(continued)

Name_____

Expressive Language Skills		Date Observed
24 to 29 Months (cont.)	Preposition *in* used. "Go in house." "Ball in box."	
	Plural used. "More cookies." "See cats."	
30 to 36 Months	Negative elements *no, can't,* and *don't* used after subject. "I can't eat." "Mommy, don't go."	
	Use of different modifiers: qualifiers (some, a lot, all one); possessives (mine, his, hers); adjectives (pretty, new, blue).	
	Overgeneralization of regular past with an "-ed." "He eated it." "I waked up."	
Language Comprehension Skills		
24 to 29 Months	Child answers routine questions (What is that? What is your name? What is [person] doing?).	
	Points to six body parts on doll or self.	
	Provides appropriate answers to yes/no questions that deal with the child's environment (Is mommy sleeping? Is daddy cooking?).	
	Comprehends pronouns: *I, my, mine, me.*	
30 to 36 Months	Follows two-step directions.	
	Provides appropriate answers for *where* (place) questions that deal with familiar information (Where does daddy work? Where do you sleep?).	
	Comprehends pronouns: *she, he, his, him, her.*	
Math Readiness Skills		
30 to 36 Months	Gives "just one" upon request.	
	Comprehends concepts *soft* and *hard* in object manipulation tasks.	
	Comprehends size concepts *big* and *tall* in object manipulation tasks.	
	Comprehends spatial concepts *on, under, out of, together,* and *away from* in object manipulation tasks.	
Social Skills		
24 to 29 Months	Likes to play near other children, but is unable to play cooperatively.	
	Becomes a grabber, and may grab desired toys away from other children.	
	Does not like to share toys.	
	Has not learned to say please but often desires the toys of other children.	
	Likes to give affection to parents.	
	May pull hair or bite before giving up a desired possession.	

(continued)

Social Skills		Date Observed
30 to 36 Months	Continues to have a strong sense of ownership but may give up a toy if offered a substitute.	
	May learn to say please if prompted.	
	Has increased desire to play near and with other children.	
	May begin cooperative play.	
	Distinguishes between boys and girls.	
	Likes to be accepted by others.	
	Enjoys hiding from others.	
	Likes to play with adults on a one-to-one basis.	
	Enjoys tumble play with other children and caregivers.	
Emotional Development Skills		
24 to 29 Months	Continues to be self-centered.	
	May exhibit increasing independence one minute and then run back to security of parents the next.	
	Likes immediate gratification of desires and finds it difficult to wait.	
	May exhibit negativism.	
	Continues to seek caregiver approval for behaviors and accomplishments.	
	Displays jealousy.	
	May develop fear of dark; needs reassurance.	
30 to 36 Months	May display negative feelings and occasional bad temper.	
	May exhibit aggressiveness.	
	May dawdle but insists on doing things for self.	
	Likes to dress self and needs praise and encouragement when correct.	
	Feels bad when reprimanded for mistakes.	
	Desires caregiver approval.	
	Wants independence but shows fear of new experiences.	
	May reveal need for clinging to security objects.	
	Needs an understanding, orderly environment.	
	May have trouble sleeping if the day's events have been emotional.	

(continued)

Name_____

■ To Review

1. List equipment you observed in the classroom that is designed to promote development of the following skills:
   Gross motor _____

   _____

   _____

   Fine motor _____

   _____

   _____

   Self-help _____

   _____

   _____

   Expressive language _____

   _____

   _____

   Language comprehension _____

   _____

   _____

   Math readiness _____

   _____

   _____

   Social _____

   _____

   _____

   Emotional _____

   _____

   _____

Observing Developmental Characteristics of Three-Year-Olds

Activity D

Chapter 5

Name _____

Date _____ Period _____

■ Objectives

After completing this activity, you will be able to
■ identify gross motor, fine motor, self-help, social-emotional, and language skills of a three-year-old child.
■ report specific information about the observation setting.

■ Preparation

1. Make arrangements to observe a three-year-old child. (More than one visit may be needed to complete the activity.)
2. Review the skills on the following charts.

■ Setting

Place _____

Address _____

Telephone number _____

Contact person _____ Title _____

Date(s) _____ Time(s) _____ to _____

_____ _____ _____

_____ _____ _____

_____ _____ _____

Child's name _____ Age _____

Description of observational setting

_____

_____

_____

Other information _____

■ To Do

As you observe the child, mark the column next to each skill the child has mastered with the month and day the skill was observed. If you wait a few months between observations, you will observe the child's progress.

Gross Motor Skills	Date Observed
Walks toe-to-heel for four steps.	
Balances on one foot for eight seconds.	
Catches a beanbag while standing.	
Performs one to three hops on one foot.	
Catches a bounced ball with hands.	

(continued)

Fine Motor Skills	Date Observed
Pours liquid from a pitcher.	
Copies a cross.	
Builds a tower of nine to ten cubes.	
Completes simple puzzles.	
Wiggles thumb.	
Folds paper twice (in imitation).	
Draws a person with three parts.	
Cuts a five-inch piece of paper in two.	
Traces a diamond.	
Cuts along a five-inch line within one-half inch of the line.	
Self-Help Skills	
Washes and dries face and hands.	
Unbuckles belt.	
Usually remains dry at night.	
Turns faucet on and off.	
Expressive Language Skills	
Preposition *on* used (book on table; sit on chair).	
Possessive ('s) used (mommy's coat; daddy's car).	
"When" questions appear.	
Negatives *cannot* and *do not* appear.	
Double negatives appear when using negative pronoun (*nobody*, *nothing*) or negative adverb (*never*, *nowhere*). Examples include "I can't do nothing" or "I don't never get to go."	
Sentences with two clauses are joined. (Then it broke and we didn't have it anymore.)	
Language Comprehension Skills	
Provides appropriate answers for "whose" questions. (Whose doll is this?)	
Provides appropriate answers for "why" (cause or reason) questions. (Why is the girl crying?)	
Provides appropriate answers for "who" (person or animal) questions. (Who lives at the North Pole?)	
Understands the pronouns *you* and *they*.	

(continued)

Language Comprehension Skills	Date Observed
Provides appropriate answers for "how" questions. (How will mother bake the pie?)	
Math Readiness Skills	
Gives "just two" upon request.	
Distinguishes between *one* and *many*.	
Understands the quantity concept *empty* in object manipulation tasks.	
Understands the concept *smaller*; points to smaller objects.	
Understands the concept *largest*; points to largest object.	
Counts while correctly pointing to three objects.	
Understands quantity concepts *full*, *more*, and *less* in object manipulation tasks.	
Comprehends spatial concepts *up*, *top*, *apart*, and *toward* in object manipulation tasks.	
Comprehends spatial concepts *around*, *in front of*, *in back of*, *high*, and *next to* in object manipulation tasks.	
Expressive Language Skills	
Is learning to share and take turns.	
Follows directions and takes pride in doing things for others.	
May act in a certain way just to please caregivers.	
Makes friends easily.	
Seeks status among peers.	
May attempt to comfort and remove cause of distress of playmates.	
Seeks friends on own initiative.	
Begins to be choosy about companions, preferring one over another.	
Uses language to make friends and to alienate others.	
Emotional Development	
Is usually cooperative, happy, and agreeable.	
Feels less frustrated because motor skills have been improved.	
May still seek comfort from caregivers when tired or hungry.	
Learns more socially acceptable ways of displaying feelings.	
May show fear of dark, animals, stories, and monsters.	

(continued)

■ To Review

1. List equipment you observed in the classroom that is designed to promote development of the following skills:

Gross motor _____

_____

_____

Fine motor _____

_____

_____

Self-help _____

_____

_____

Expressive language _____

_____

_____

Language comprehension _____

_____

_____

Math readiness _____

_____

_____

Social _____

_____

_____

Emotional _____

_____

_____

Understanding Four- and Five-Year-Olds

Observing Four- and Five-Year-Olds

Activity A

Chapter 6

Name _____

Date _____ Period _____

■ Objectives

After completing this activity, you will be able to
- observe the appearance of a four-year-old and/or a five-year-old child.
- observe the child's development.
- describe the types of activities for which the child needed assistance from an adult.

■ Preparation

1. Make arrangements to observe a four-year-old and/or five-year-old child in a child care or preschool program.
2. Review the developmental characteristics described in the textbook.

■ Setting

Place _____

Address _____

Telephone number _____

Contact person_____ Title _____

Date _____ Time _____ to _____

Child's name _____ Birthdate _____

Age_____ Height _____ Weight _____

Other information _____

_____

_____

■ To Do

Respond to the items listed below during your observation of the child.

Physical Development

1. Describe the child's physical appearance.

_____

_____

_____

(continued)

2. How do the child's height and weight compare with other children the same age?

_____

_____

_____

_____

_____

Motor Skills

3. Describe the child's fine motor and gross motor skills.

_____

_____

_____

_____

_____

4. Compare the child's motor skills with those expected at this age. (Refer to the textbook if needed.)

_____

_____

_____

_____

_____

Cognitive Development

5. What evidence of the child's thinking processes have you observed?

_____

_____

_____

_____

_____

Language Development

6. Describe the child's language skills.

_____

_____

_____

_____

_____

(continued)

Social-Emotional Development

7. Describe the child's social and emotional development.

_____

_____

_____

_____

_____

8. How does the child compare with the other children in the same age group?

_____

_____

_____

_____

_____

Self-Help Skills

9. Describe the self-help skills that this child was able to do. Provide specific examples.

_____

_____

_____

_____

_____

General Characteristics

10. Describe the child's behavior. Note whether it was typical or atypical of children this age.

_____

_____

_____

_____

_____

Development of Four- and Five-Year-Olds

Activity B

Chapter 6

Name _____

Date _____ Period _____

Objectives

After completing this activity, you will be able to
- observe general characteristics of four-year-old and/or five-year-old children.
- recall the children's physical, social, emotional, and cognitive development.
- describe the types of activities that the children seem to enjoy.
- describe the relationships of the children with one another and adults.

Preparation

1. Make arrangements to observe a group of four-year-olds and/or five-year-olds in a child care, preschool, or Head Start program.
2. Review the developmental characteristics given in the textbook.

Setting

Place _____

Address _____

Telephone number _____

Contact person_____ Title _____

Date _____ Time _____ to _____

Number of children _____ Number of adults _____

Other information _____

_____

_____

To Do

Observe the group of children for at least one hour. Then answer the questions listed below.

1. Describe incidents or examples of general characteristics of four-year-olds and/or five-year-olds listed in the text that you observed.

_____

_____

_____

_____

_____

_____

_____

_____

(continued)

2. List the physical skills and motor behaviors the children demonstrated.

_____

_____

_____

_____

_____

_____

_____

_____

_____

_____

_____

3. Describe the relationships of the children with one another and the adults.

_____

_____

_____

_____

_____

_____

_____

_____

_____

_____

_____

4. Describe the types of activities the children appeared to enjoy.

_____

_____

_____

_____

_____

_____

_____

_____

_____

Observing Developmental Characteristics of Four-Year-Olds

Activity C

Chapter 6

Name _____

Date _____ Period _____

■ Objectives

After completing this activity, you will be able to
- ■ identify gross motor, fine motor, self-help, social, and language skills of a four-year-old child.
- ■ report specific information about the observation setting.

■ Preparation

1. Make arrangements to observe a four-year-old child. (More than one visit may be needed to complete the activity.)
2. Review the skills on the following chart.

■ Setting

Place _____

Address _____

Telephone number _____

Contact person_____ Title _____

Date(s) _____Time(s) _____to _____

_____ _____ _____

_____ _____ _____

_____ _____ _____

Child's name _____ Birthdate _____

Description of observational setting _____

_____

_____

_____

Other information _____

■ To Do

As you observe the child, mark the column next to each skill that the child has mastered with the month and day the skill was observed. If you wait a few months between observations, you will observe the child's progress.

Gross Motor Skills	Date Observed
Catches beanbag with hands.	
Hops on one foot.	
Walks down stairs with alternating feet.	
Throws ball overhand.	
Carries a cup of liquid without spilling.	

(continued)

Gross Motor Skills	Date Observed
Rides bicycle with training wheels.	
Balances on one foot for 10 seconds.	
Skips with alternating feet.	
Walks backward toe-to-heel for four consecutive steps.	
Builds elaborate structures with blocks.	
Fine Motor Skills	
Builds a three-block bridge from a model.	
Completes a six- to eight-piece puzzle.	
Folds paper diagonally (three folds).	
Copies a square.	
Paints and draws freely.	
Self-Help Skills	
Laces shoes.	
Buckles belt.	
Cuts with knife.	
Dresses and undresses with supervision.	
Distinguishes front and back of clothing.	
Zips separating zipper.	
Language Skills	
Understands *has/doesn't have* and *is/is not.*	
Identifies penny, nickel, and dime.	
Follows three commands in proper order (clear the table, wash the table, and get ready to go outdoors).	
Understands the pronoun *we.*	
Uses irregular verb forms (ate, ran, went).	
Uses regular tense (ed) verbs.	
Uses third person present tense verbs (runs, shops).	
Speaks fluently with a 1500-word vocabulary.	
Uses sentences of four to eight words.	

(continued)

Name_____

Language Skills (cont.)	Date Observed
Asks many *when*, *why*, and *how* questions.	
Tells simple jokes.	
Math Readiness Skills	
Understands the concepts *beside*, *bottom*, *backward*, and *forward* in object manipulation tasks.	
Understands size concepts *short*, *fat*, and *thin* in object manipulation tasks.	
Counts one to four chips and correctly answers questions such as "How many in all?" with cardinal number.	
Says correct number when shown two to six objects and asked "How many?"	
Can rote count one through nine.	
Understands the concepts of *triangle* and *circle*.	
Understands the concepts *tallest* and *same size*.	
Social-Emotional Development	
May seem less pleasant and cooperative than at age three.	
May be more moody, tries to express emotions verbally.	
Strives for independence; resents being treated like a baby.	
May be stubborn and quarrelsome at times.	
Resents directions; may think he or she knows and can do it all.	
Learns to ask for things instead of snatching things from others.	
Is increasingly aware of attitudes and asks for approval.	
Needs and seeks parental approval often.	
Has strong sense of family and home.	
May quote parents and boast about parents to friends.	
Becomes more interested in friends than in adults.	
Shares possessions and toys, especially with special friends.	
Suggests taking turns but may be unable to wait for his or her own turn.	
Likes to play with friends in cooperative play activities.	

(continued)

■ To Review

1. List equipment you observed in the classroom that is designed to promote development of the following skills:

Gross motor _____

_____

_____

Fine motor _____

_____

_____

Self-help _____

_____

_____

Expressive language _____

_____

_____

Language comprehension _____

_____

_____

Math readiness_____

_____

_____

Social_____

_____

_____

Emotional _____

_____

_____

Observing Developmental Characteristics of Five-Year-Olds

Activity D

Chapter 6

Name _____

Date _____ Period _____

■ Objectives

After completing this activity, you will be able to
■ identify gross motor, fine motor, self-help, social, and language skills of a five-year-old child.
■ report specific information about the observation setting.

■ Preparation

1. Make arrangements to observe a five-year-old child. (More than one visit may be needed to complete the activity.)
2. Review the skills on the following chart.

■ Setting

Place _____

Address _____

Telephone number _____

Contact person _____ Title _____

Date(s) _____ Time(s) _____ to _____

_____   _____   _____

_____   _____   _____

_____   _____   _____

Child's name _____ Birthdate _____

Description of observational setting _____

_____

_____

_____

Other information _____

■ To Do

As you observe the child, mark the column next to each skill that the child has mastered with the month and day the skill was observed. If you wait a few months between observations, you will observe the child's progress.

Gross Motor Skills	Date Observed
Marches to music.	
Jumps from table height.	
Climbs fences.	
Attempts to jump rope.	
Attempts to skate.	

(continued)

Gross Motor Skills	Date Observed
Walks forward, backward, and sideways on balance beam.	
Uses hands to catch ball.	
Fine Motor Skills	
Copies a triangle.	
Prints first name.	
Prints simple words.	
Dials telephone numbers correctly.	
Models objects with clay.	
Colors within lines.	
Draws recognizable people, houses, and vehicles.	
Self-Help Skills	
Dresses and undresses without assistance.	
Washes self.	
Puts shoes on correct feet.	
Unbuttons back buttons.	
Language Skills	
Uses third person irregular verbs. (He has a ball.)	
Uses compound sentences. (I went to the grocery store and I went to my grandmother's house.)	
Uses descriptions in telling a story.	
Uses some pronouns correctly.	
Uses words to describe sizes, distances, weather, time, and location.	
Asks the meaning of words.	
Recalls the main details of a story.	
Recognizes some verbal absurdities.	
Tells original stories.	
Has a 2000-word vocabulary.	
Math Readiness Skills	
Understands *square* and *rectangle*.	
Understands the concept of *same shape*.	

(continued)

Math Readiness Skills	Date Observed
Understands the position concepts *first* and *last* in object manipulation tasks.	
Understands position concept *middle*.	
Rote counts 1 through 20.	
Recognizes the numerals 1 through 10.	
Writes the numerals 1 through 5.	
May count 1 to 20 objects correctly.	
Social-Emotional Development	
Shows increased willingness to cooperate.	
Is more patient, generous, and conscientious.	
Expresses anger verbally rather than physically.	
Is more reasonable when in a quarrel.	
Develops a sense of fairness.	
Likes supervision, accepts instructions, and asks permission.	
Has a strong desire to please parents and other adults.	
Still depends on parents for emotional support and approval.	
Is proud of mother and father.	
Delights in helping parents.	
May act protective of younger siblings.	
Shapes ideas of gender roles by watching parents' behavior.	
Is increasingly social and talkative.	
Is eager to make friends and develop strong friendships.	
May pick a best friend.	
Prefers cooperative play in small groups.	
Prefers friends of same age and gender.	
Stays with play groups as long as interests hold.	
Learns to respect the property of friends.	

(continued)

■ To Review

1. List equipment you observed in the classroom that is designed to promote development of the following skills:

Gross motor _____

_____

_____

Fine motor _____

_____

_____

Self-help _____

_____

_____

Expressive language _____

_____

_____

Language comprehension _____

_____

_____

Math readiness _____

_____

_____

Social _____

_____

_____

Emotional _____

_____

_____

Middle Childhood

Observing Six- and Seven-Year-Olds

Activity A

Chapter 7

Name _____

Date _____ **Period** _____

■ Objectives

After completing this activity, you will be able to
- ■ observe the physical appearance of a six- or seven-year-old child.
- ■ observe the development of a six- or seven-year-old.
- ■ describe the types of activities for which the child needed adult assistance.

■ Preparation

1. Make arrangements to observe a six- or seven-year-old child in an elementary school or during after-school child care.
2. Review the developmental characteristics of a child this age as described in the textbook.

■ Setting

Place _____

Address _____

Telephone number _____

Contact person_____ Title _____

Date _____ Time _____ to _____

Child's name _____ Birthdate _____

Age_____ Height _____ Weight _____

Other information _____

_____

■ To Do

Respond to the items listed below during your observation of the child.

Physical Development

1. Describe the child's physical appearance.

_____

_____

_____

_____

(continued)

2. How do the child's weight and height compare with other children the same age?

_____

_____

_____

_____

Motor Skills

3. Describe the child's fine motor and gross motor skills.

_____

_____

_____

_____

4. Compare the child's motor skills with those expected at this age.

_____

_____

_____

_____

Cognitive Development

5. What evidence of the child's thinking processes have you observed?

_____

_____

_____

_____

Language Development

6. Describe the child's language skills.

_____

_____

_____

_____

Social-Emotional Development

7. Describe the child's social and emotional development.

_____

_____

_____

_____

(continued)

8. How does the child compare with other children in the same age group?

_____

_____

_____

General Characteristics

9. Describe the child's behavior. Note whether it appears typical or atypical of children this age.

_____

_____

_____

_____

Observing Eight- and Nine-Year-Olds

Activity B

Chapter 7

Name _____

Date _____ Period _____

■ Objectives

After completing this activity, you will be able to
- observe general characteristics of eight-year-old and nine-year-old children.
- recall the children's physical, social, emotional, and cognitive development.
- describe the types of activities the children seem to enjoy.
- describe the relationship of the children with one another and adults.
- describe any gender differences noted between boys and girls.

■ Preparation

1. Make arrangements to observe a group of eight- and nine-year-old children in a local elementary school or during after-school child care.
2. Review the development of a child this age as described in the textbook.

■ Setting

Place _____

Address _____

Telephone number_____

Contact person_____ Title _____

Date _____ Time _____ to _____

Number of children _____ Number of adults_____

Other information _____

_____

■ To Do

Observe the group of children for at least one hour. Then answer the questions below.

1. Describe incidents or examples of general characteristics of eight- and nine-year-olds listed in the text that you observed.

_____

_____

_____

_____

_____

_____

_____

_____

_____

_____

(continued)

2. List the physical skills and motor behaviors the children demonstrated.

_____

_____

_____

_____

_____

3. Describe the relationship of the children with one another and adults.

_____

_____

_____

_____

_____

_____

_____

4. Describe the types of activities the children seemed to enjoy.

_____

_____

_____

_____

_____

_____

_____

5. Describe any gender differences in activity preferences and social relationships between the girls and boys that you observed.

_____

_____

_____

_____

Observing Ten- and Eleven-Year-Olds

Activity C

Chapter 7

Name _____

Date _____ Period _____

■ Objectives

After completing this activity, you will be able to
■ observe general characteristics of ten-year-old and eleven-year-old children.
■ recall the children's physical, social, emotional, and cognitive development.
■ describe the types of activities the children seem to enjoy.
■ describe the relationship of the children with one another and adults.
■ describe any gender differences noted between the boys and the girls.

■ Preparation

1. Make arrangements to observe a group of ten- and eleven-year-old children in a local elementary school or during after-school child care.
2. Review the development of a child this age as described in the textbook.

■ Setting

Place _____

Address _____

Telephone number _____

Contact person_____ Title _____

Date _____ Time _____ to _____

Number of children _____ Number of adults _____

Other information _____

_____

■ To Do

Observe the group of children for at least one hour. Then answer the questions below.

1. Describe incidents or examples of general characteristics of ten- and eleven-year-olds listed in the text that you observed.

_____

_____

_____

_____

_____

_____

_____

_____

_____

_____

(continued)

2. List the physical skills and motor behaviors the children demonstrated.

_____

_____

_____

_____

_____

_____

3. Describe the relationship of the children with one another and adults.

_____

_____

_____

_____

_____

_____

_____

_____

4. Describe the types of activities the children seemed to enjoy.

_____

_____

_____

_____

_____

_____

_____

5. Describe any gender differences in activity preferences and social relationships between the girls and boys that you observed.

_____

_____

_____

_____

Preparing the Environment

Center Physical Space

Activity A

Chapter 8

Name _____

Date _____ Period_____

■ Objectives

After completing this activity, you will be able to
■ draw and describe the physical space of a child care center.
■ explain the locations of the general center areas.

■ Preparation

1. Make arrangements to visit a child care, preschool, Head Start, or kindergarten early childhood program.
2. You will need a pencil, ruler, and tape measure to use when drawing the floor plan.

■ Setting

Place _____

Address _____

Telephone number_____

Contact person_____ Title _____

Date _____

Number of children enrolled_____ Size of staff _____

Other information _____

_____

_____

■ To Do

On the graph paper provided, draw a floor plan of the early childhood facilities. Include the following general areas:
1. entrance
2. director's office
3. isolation area
4. kitchen or kitchenette
5. staff room (if available)
6. classrooms
7. bathrooms

Then evaluate the plan by answering the questions that follow.

(continued)

Name_____

Center Floor Plan

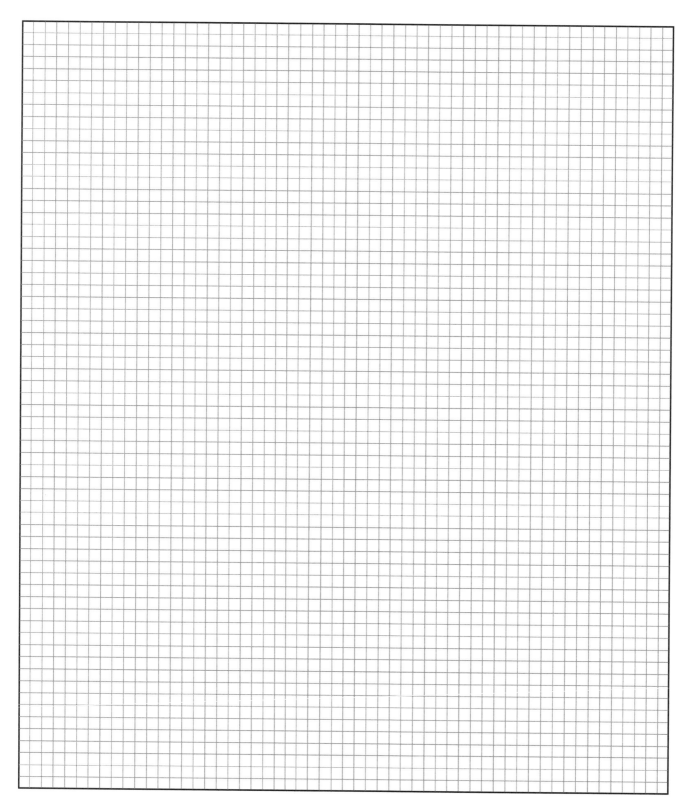

Scale: 1/8 inch = 1 foot

(continued)

Name_____

■ To Review

1. **Entrance:** Describe the entrance. Was it appealing and attractive? If not, how could it be improved?

_____

_____

_____

_____

2. **Director's Office:** Describe the location of the director's office. Was it in a convenient location? If not, where would it be more conveniently located?

_____

_____

_____

_____

3. **Isolation Area:** Describe the location of the isolation area. Could this area be improved? Explain. _____

_____

_____

_____

_____

4. **Kitchen:** Describe the location of the kitchen. Was it in a convenient location? If not, where could it be more conveniently located?

_____

_____

_____

_____

5. **Bathroom(s):** Describe the location of the bathroom(s). Was it (were they) conveniently located adjacent to the playroom(s)?

_____

_____

_____

_____

Classroom Physical Space

Activity B

Chapter 8

Name _____

Date _____ Period _____

■ Objectives

After completing this activity, you will be able to
- ■ draw the space arrangement of a classroom (playroom) in a child care center or kindergarten.
- ■ explain the positioning of activity areas in the room observed.

■ Preparation

1. Make arrangements to visit an early childhood program.
2. You will need a pencil, ruler, and measuring tape to use when drawing the floor plan.

■ Setting

Place _____

Address _____

Telephone number _____

Contact person_____ Title _____

Date _____

Number of children in classroom _____ Number of teachers _____

Other information _____

_____

■ To Do

On the graph paper provided, draw the floor plan of the room. Label all the activity areas. Then evaluate the floor plan of the room using the questions below.

■ To Review

1. Is there a minimum of 35 square feet per child? _____

2. Were there individual lockers for each child?_____

3. Were the shelving units designed or selected in relationship to the height of the children? _____

4. Are activity areas arranged logically? Explain. _____

_____

_____

_____

_____

_____

_____

(continued)

Classroom Arrangement

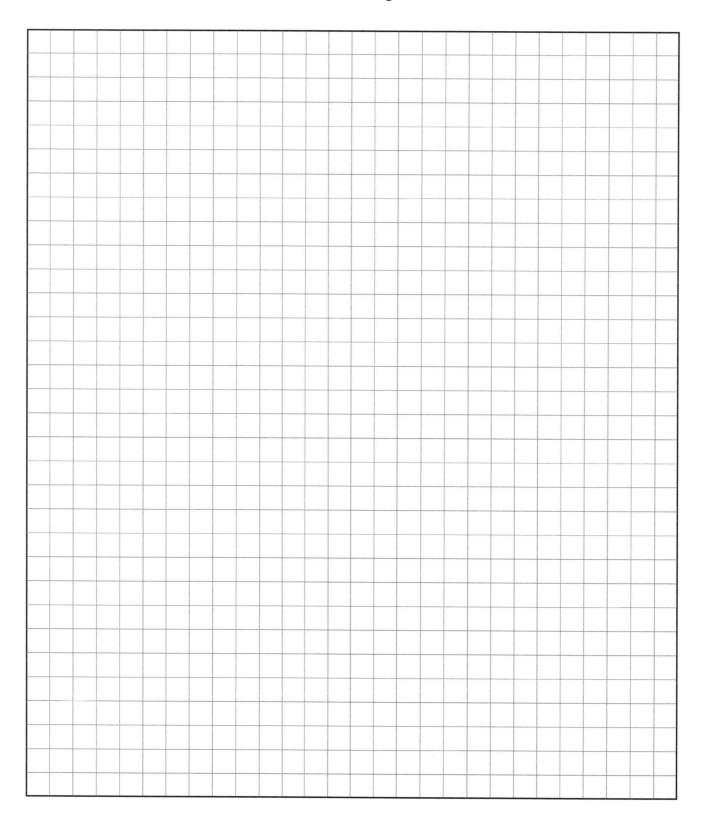

Scale: ¼ inch = 1 foot

Goals and Space

Activity C

Chapter 8

Name _____

Date _____ Period _____

■ Objectives

After completing this activity, you will be able to
- ■ discuss classroom goals with a director or teacher.
- ■ observe and record how the environment supports each goal.

■ Preparation

1. Make arrangements to visit an early childhood classroom.
2. Before the visit, ask the teacher or director to share the classroom goals. Record them in the space provided on the chart on the next page.

■ Setting

Place _____

Address _____

Telephone number _____

Contact person_____ Title _____

Date _____ Time _____ to _____

Number of children _____ Ages_____ Number of teachers _____

Other information _____

_____

_____

■ To Do

As you observe the classroom setting, record how the room arrangement supports the classroom goals. An example is given below.

Goals and Space

Center goals for children	Room arrangement
To promote independence.	*Furniture scaled to children.* *Hooks are installed in lockers so they are accessible to children.* *Bookcase has low shelves allowing children to remove books from top shelf without assistance.* *Storage is provided for each child.*

(continued)

Name_____

Goals and Space

Center goals for children	Room arrangement

Maintaining the Environment

Activity D

Chapter 8

Name _____

Date _____ Period _____

■ Objectives

After completing this activity, you will be able to
■ identify the responsibilities of teachers in maintaining classroom space.
■ discuss the use of time in maintaining the classroom.
■ explain the importance of maintaining an ordered environment.

■ Preparation

1. Arrange to visit a child care, preschool, Head Start, or kindergarten program. Plan to be there before the children arrive.
2. Review the maintenance criteria checklist beginning on this page.

■ Setting

Place _____

Address _____

Telephone number _____

Contact person_____ Title _____

Name of person observed _____

Individual's position _____

Date _____ Time _____ to _____

Other information _____

■ To Do

Evaluate the maintenance of the environment using the checklist below. Then answer the questions that follow with the help of the teacher present.

Activity Area Responsibilities	Done
Blockbuilding area	
A. Clear and dust tops of shelves.	
B. Separate and stack blocks according to size.	
C. Place small transportation toys neatly on the shelves.	
Art area	
A. Wash easels and brushes thoroughly after each use.	
B. Check that supplies on storage shelves are orderly.	
C. Clean tops of shelves. (Some may need daily dusting.)	

(continued)

Activity Area Responsibilities

	Done
D. Check each shelf and tray for organization.	
E. Wash spattered paint from floors, walls, and tables.	
F. Put children's artwork in their cubbies.	
G. Wipe off excess paints from children's smocks and paint rack on daily basis.	
H. Refill and clean paint jars as needed.	
Dramatic play area	
A. Organize dress-up clothes.	
B. Organize dolls and doll bedding.	
C. Check all shelving for neatness and organization.	
D. Wash toy dishes on a weekly basis or as needed.	
E. Check play refrigerator daily to remove old play dough.	
Sensory area	
A. Clean out and wash sensory table thoroughly after each use.	
B. Check that supplies are put away orderly.	
C. Sweep and/or wash any spilled sensory materials daily.	
D. Wipe sensory materials from children's smocks as needed.	
Woodworking area	
A. Hang tools and safety goggles neatly.	
B. Place wood scraps in boxes, sorting by size.	
C. Sweep or vacuum any sawdust, wood chips, nails, etc., daily.	
Sleeping area	
A. Fold blankets neatly.	
B. Stack cots or mats neatly.	
C. Wash and/or change linens weekly or as needed.	
Small manipulative area	
A. Clear all papers, toys, and all other items from tops of shelves.	
B. Sort small manipulative materials each day and place in their proper trays.	

(continued)

Activity Area Responsibilities

	Done
C. Place trays individually on gliders/shelves.	
D. Check puzzles daily for missing pieces. Report missing pieces to the head teacher or director.	
Book area	
A. Remove and repair all damaged books.	
B. Place books neatly on the shelves.	
C. Rotate books as needed.	
Music area	
A. Keep top of piano neat and free from clutter.	
B. Stack or place music instruments and equipment on shelves.	
C. Replace tapes or CDs in their proper cases.	
D. Double-check at the end of program to make sure tape or CD player is turned off.	
Science area	
A. Organize and dust science table(s) daily.	
B. Clean aquarium or other animal cages as needed.	
C. Feed pets and water plants as needed.	
Eating area	
A. Wash tables and chairs daily.	
B. Sweep and wash floor daily.	
Lockers or clothes cart	
A. Place clothing neatly in the children's lockers.	
B. Return name tags to a shelf or a basket.	
C. Clear tops of lockers and dust if necessary.	
Kitchen area and storage room	
A. Straighten and clean counters daily.	
B. Scour sinks daily.	
C. Organize cupboards; dust once each week.	
D. Notify the director or cook when supplies are needed.	

(continued)

Activity Area Responsibilities

	Done
E. Remove soiled dish towels and dishcloths on a daily basis.	
F. Remove nonfood items from the refrigerator.	
Care of carpeting	
A. Clean spots of paint, milk, paste, or food immediately.	
B. Report all spots to the janitor or director.	
Outdoor	
A. Pick up all litter including paper, cans, and twigs daily.	
B. Return all movable equipment to the classroom or storage shed after outdoor playtime.	

■ To Review

1. Approximately how much daily and weekly time is spent on center maintenance?

_____

_____

2. What guidelines can be used to assure that maintenance time is spent as efficiently as possible?

_____

_____

_____

_____

_____

_____

3. How does order/lack of order affect the daily functioning of this center?

_____

_____

_____

_____

_____

_____

_____

Play Yard Space

Name _____

Date _____ **Period** _____

■ Objectives

After completing this activity, you will be able to
■ draw an outdoor play area.
■ explain the positioning of the play equipment and space in the area observed.

■ Preparation

1. Make arrangements to visit an early childhood center with an outdoor play area.
2. You will need a pencil, ruler, and tape measure.

■ Setting

Place _____

Address _____

Telephone number _____

Contact person_____ Title _____

Date _____ Time _____ to _____

Number of students enrolled _____ Size of staff _____

Other information _____

_____

_____

■ To Do

On the graph paper provided, draw the shape of the outdoor activity area. Then draw in all the outdoor equipment and surface paths present. Evaluate the space by answering the questions that follow.

(continued)

Name_____

Play Yard Arrangement

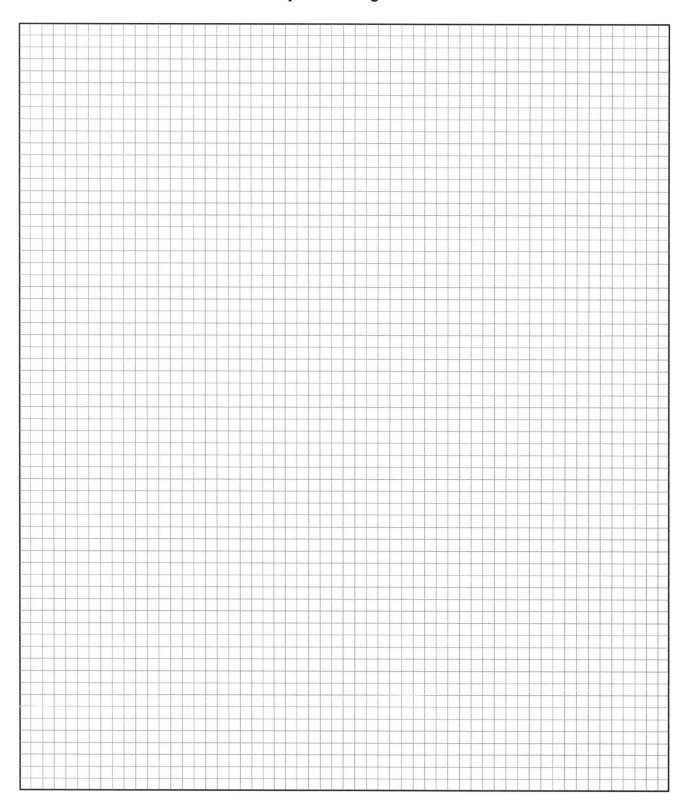

scale: 1/8 inch = 1 foot

(continued)

■ **To Review**

1. Describe the play yard surface. Was it appropriate or inappropriate for use with young children? Explain.

_____

_____

_____

_____

_____

_____

2. Describe the fencing used. Explain why it was or was not aesthetically pleasing. _____

_____

_____

_____

_____

_____

_____

3. Was landscaping used to make the play yard aesthetically pleasing? If used, describe. _____

_____

_____

_____

_____

_____

4. Were surface paths included for the children to drive or ride wheeled toys? If so, describe their locations.

_____

_____

_____

_____

_____

Name_____

5. Was the stationary equipment placed in the best location? Explain. _____

_____

_____

_____

_____

_____

6. Was the sandbox placed in a shady area? If not, how could the children be protected from the sun? _____

_____

_____

_____

_____

_____

_____

Selecting Toys, Equipment, and Educational Materials

Evaluating a Toy

Activity A

Chapter 9

Name _____

Date _____ Period_____

■ Objectives

After completing this activity, you will be able to
■ observe a child interacting with a piece of equipment.
■ evaluate a toy.

■ Preparation

1. Arrange to visit an early childhood classroom.
2. Select a toy to evaluate.
3. Review the criteria listed below for evaluating a toy.

■ Setting

Place _____

Address _____

Telephone number _____

Contact person_____ Title _____

Date _____ Time _____ to _____

Other information _____

_____

■ To Do

Observe a child interacting with the piece of equipment. Use the criteria listed below to evaluate the toy. Then answer the question that follows.

Evaluating a Toy	Yes	No
1. Does it complement program goals?		
2. Does it add balance to existing materials and equipment?		

(continued)

Evaluating a Toy

	Yes	No
3. Can it be used in available classroom space?		
4. Does it require a great deal of supervision?		
5. Is it easy to maintain?		
6. Is it durable?		
7. Is there sufficient quantity?		
8. Does it require the child's involvement?		
9. Is it developmentally appropriate?		
10. Is it nonviolent?		
11. Is it nonsexist?		
12. Is it multicultural?		
13. Is it safe?		

■ To Review

1. Would you purchase this toy for your classroom? Justify your answer.

_____

_____

_____

_____

_____

_____

Evaluating a Swing Set

Activity B

Chapter 9

Name _____

Date _____ Period _____

■ Objectives

After completing this activity, you will be able to
- identify safety features of a swing set.
- evaluate a swing set.

■ Preparation

1. Make arrangements to visit a children's play area that contains a swing set.
2. Review the evaluation criteria on the checklist below.

■ Setting

Place _____

Address _____

Telephone number _____

Contact person_____ Title _____

Date _____ Time _____ to _____

Other information _____

_____

_____

■ To Do

Evaluate the swing set using the criteria listed below. Then answer the questions that follow.

Evaluating a Swing Set

	Yes	No
1. Is the construction durable?		
2. Is it an appropriate height?		
3. Does it complement existing equipment in function?		
4. Are the exercise rings under 5 inches or over 10 inches in diameter?		
5. Are the S-rings closed?		

(continued)

Evaluating a Swing Set

	Yes	No
6. Are the swing seats plastic or canvas?		
7. Is it free of exposed nuts and bolts?		
8. Is it free of sharp edges?		
9. Can the equipment be properly anchored?		
10. Is the equipment easy to maintain?		

■ To Review

1. Would you purchase this swing set? Justify your answer.

_____

_____

_____

_____

_____

_____

2. Could this piece of equipment be improved by the manufacturer? If so, explain.

_____

_____

_____

_____

Learning Skills and Toys

Activity C

Chapter 9

Name _____

Date _____ Period _____

■ Objectives

After completing this activity, you will be able to
■ evaluate the learning skills promoted by five different toys.
■ explain the value of each of the five toys.
■ discuss the differences among the five toys.

■ Preparation

Gather a ball, puzzle, book, toy gun, and blocks.

■ Setting

Place _____

Time _____

Other information _____

■ To Do

Review the skills listed on the chart below. Then evaluate each of the five toys by placing a check mark next to the skills promoted by each toy. Finally, answer the questions to evaluate the toys.

Learning Skills and Toys

	blocks	ball	puzzle	book	toy gun
auditory discrimination					
balance					
color concepts					
counting					
fine motor development					
hand-eye coordination					
hearing skills					
language concepts					
gross motor development					

(continued)

Name_____

Learning Skills and Toys

	blocks	ball	puzzle	book	toy gun
matching concepts					
number concepts					
patterning					
seeing skills					
self-concept					
self-image					
sensory discrimination					
sequencing					
social skills					
space perception					
strength					
throwing and catching					
visual discrimination					

■ To Review

1. Which toy promotes the *most* skills? _____

2. Which toy promotes the *least* skills? _____

3. Considering the skills promoted, rank the toys from most useful (1) to least useful (5).

_____ blocks

_____ ball

_____ puzzle

_____ book

_____ toy gun

Multicultural Checklist

Name _____

Date _____ Period_____

■ Objectives

After completing this activity, you will be able to
■ identify items that represent a variety of cultural and ethnic groups.
■ evaluate a classroom environment for multicultural toys and materials.

■ Preparation

1. Arrange to visit a child care, preschool, Head Start, or kindergarten program.
2. Review the multicultural checklist.

■ Setting

Place _____

Address _____

Telephone number_____

Contact person_____ Title _____

Date _____ Time _____ to _____

Other information _____

_____

_____

■ To Do

Using the checklist, evaluate the presence of multicultural toys and material in the environment. Then answer the question that follows.

Multicultural Checklist

Items for Identity Development	Yes	No
A variety of books containing accurate information about many cultures		
Puppets and dolls representing various ethnic and cultural backgrounds		
Puzzles and small manipulatives representing people from around the world		
Colors of art materials and supplies reflecting a variety of skin tones		
Posters and pictures representing diversity		
Instruments and music representing the children's cultural backgrounds		
Dress-up clothing and cooking utensils for the dramatic play area representing various cultures		

(continued)

■ **To Review**

1. What multicultural toys and materials need to be provided in this classroom to promote the children's sense of identity? Explain.

_____

_____

_____

_____

_____

_____

_____

_____

_____

2. What strengths do you recognize among the program's toys in regard to multiculturalism?

_____

_____

_____

_____

_____

_____

_____

_____

_____

Promoting Children's Safety

Indoor Safety Checklist

Activity A

Chapter 10

Name _____

Date _____ **Period** _____

■ Objectives

After completing this activity, you will be able to
- ■ check for important indoor safety precautions in a child care setting.
- ■ identify items that are important for maintaining a safe indoor environment for children.

■ Preparation

1. Arrange to visit a child care, preschool, Head Start, or kindergarten program.
2. Review the safety criteria outlined on the checklist below.

■ Setting

Place _____

Address _____

Telephone number _____

Contact person_____ Title _____

Date _____ Time _____ to _____

Other information _____

■ To Do

Using the criteria listed, observe to see if the center meets adequate safety conditions. Check the appropriate column. Then answer the questions that follow.

Safety Checklist

	Yes	No
1. Exit passageways and exits are free from furniture and equipment.		
2. Locks on bathroom doors and toilet stalls can be opened from the outside and are readily accessible to center staff.		
3. Protective receptacle covers are on all electrical outlets.		
4. Permanent wiring is installed rather than lengthy extension cords.		
5. Each wall outlet contains no more than two electrical appliances.		

(continued)

Indoor Safety Checklist	Yes	No
6. Monthly staff inspections are conducted on facilities.		
7. A fire evacuation plan is posted.		
8. Fire drills are scheduled on a monthly basis.		
9. Flammable, combustible, and dangerous materials are marked and stored in areas accessible only to staff.		
10. Children are restricted to floors with grade level exits (no stairs).		
11. The basement door is kept closed.		
12. There is no storage under stairs.		
13. Fire extinguishers are in place and checked regularly.		
14. Smoke alarms and fire alarms are working properly.		
15. Fire alarm system meets local regulations.		
16. Premises are clean indicating housekeeping is maintained.		
17. Dangerous pieces of equipment (knives, scissors, etc.) are kept out of the reach of children.		
18. The hot water heater is set low enough so children are not burned while washing their hands.		
19. Medicine, poisonous substances, and the first aid kit are kept out of the reach of young children.		
20. Floors are kept clean of spills and litter.		
21. Stairway handrails are at children's height.		
22. Lighting on stairways is adequate.		
23. Stairs are covered with a nonslip surface.		
24. Emergency information for staff and children is near phone.		
25. Storage units are stable and secure against sliding or falling over.		
26. Strict sanitary procedures are followed during food preparation.		

■ To Review

1. Did the center meet all the safety criteria? _____

2. If not, describe what center personnel must do to make the environment safer for children.

_____

_____

_____

_____

_____

Outdoor Safety Checklist

Activity B

Chapter 10

Name _____

Date _____ Period _____

■ Objectives

After completing this activity, you will be able to
- ■ check for important outdoor safety precautions in a child care setting.
- ■ identify items that are important for maintaining a safe outdoor environment for children.

■ Preparation

1. Arrange to visit a center with an outdoor play yard designed for preschool children.
2. Review the criteria outlined on the checklist below.

■ Setting

Place _____

Address _____

Telephone number _____

Contact person _____ Title _____

Date _____ Time _____ to _____

Number of children _____ Ages _____

Other information _____

■ To Do

Using the criteria listed, observe to see if the play yard meets adequate safety conditions. Then answer the questions that follow.

Outdoor Safety Checklist

	Yes	No
1. Play yard is fenced.		
2. If a gate is provided, the lock is in good condition.		
3. Surfaces are free from clutter.		
4. Equipment is age appropriate.		
5. Construction of equipment is durable.		
6. Nuts and bolts are covered to prevent injury.		
7. Sharp edges on equipment are filed.		
8. The equipment is properly anchored.		
9. S-rings are closed.		

(continued)

Outdoor Safety Checklist (Cont.)

	Yes	No
10. Cushioned surfaces are under play structures.		
11. Shade is available.		
12. Plants, shrubs, and trees are free from thorns or sharp edges.		
13. Plants, shrubs, and flowers are nonpoisonous.		
14. Sand area is covered when not in use.		
15. Sand is free from insects and animal litter.		
16. Water is drained from outdoor table when not in use.		

■ To Review

1. Did the play yard meet all the safety criteria? _____

2. If not, describe what personnel must do to make the environment safer for children.

_____

_____

_____

_____

_____

_____

_____

_____

_____

_____

_____

_____

_____

_____

_____

_____

_____

_____

_____

_____

Planning Nutritious Meals and Snacks

Serving Adequate Meals

Activity A

Chapter 11

Name _____

Date _____ Period _____

■ Objectives

After completing this activity, you will be able to
■ evaluate the serving sizes of items served for breakfast or lunch at a child care center.
■ evaluate the menu served on the basis of the Food Guide Pyramid for Young Children.

■ Preparation

1. Make arrangements to visit a child care center or kindergarten program in a private or public setting. Plan to be there during breakfast or lunch.
2. Review the text and complete the recommended serving sizes for the age you will observe in the chart below.

■ Setting

Place _____

Address _____

Telephone number _____

Contact person _____ Title _____

Date _____ Time _____ to _____

Number of children _____ Age _____

Other information _____

■ To Do

Observe the serving of breakfast or lunch. Record the foods served in the chart below. Then evaluate the meal by answering the questions that follow.

Food	Serving Size	Recommended serving size for age
Milk		
Bread		
Cereal		
Vegetable		
Fruit		

(continued)

Food	Serving Size	Recommended serving size for age
Meat		
Egg		
Dried peas or beans, cooked		
Peanut butter		
Cheese		
Cottage cheese		
Butter or margarine		

List the menu items served according to the food groups in the Food Guide Pyramid for Young Children.

Grain group: _____

_____

Vegetable group: _____

_____

Fruit group: _____

_____

Meat group: _____

_____

Milk group: _____

_____

Fats and sweets group: _____

_____

■ To Review

1. Were all food groups adequately represented? If not, how could the menu be improved?

_____

_____

2. Were the children provided adequate serving sizes? Explain.

_____

_____

Guiding Children's Health

Staff Health Practices

Activity A

Chapter 12

Name _____

Date _____ Period_____

■ Objectives

After completing this activity, you will be able to
- ■ identify health practices that prevent food contamination and foodborne illness.
- ■ describe practices that need to be followed to prevent growth of bacteria and protect children's health.

■ Preparation

1. Arrange to visit a child care center during a time when food is being prepared.
2. Read through the checklist of health practices below.

■ Setting

Place _____

Address _____

Telephone number_____

Contact person_____ Title _____

Date _____ Time _____ to _____

Other information _____

■ To Do

As you observe food preparation, check *not observed, yes,* or *no* for each health practice. (If you cannot arrange to observe the food preparation process, ask the cook or director whether each practice is followed.)

Staff Health Practices

Health Practices	Not Observed	Yes	No
1. Adults and children wash hands thoroughly after each visit to the bathroom.			
2. Hands are washed after coughing, sneezing, rubbing nose, or handling tissues.			
3. Disposable tissues are used.			

(continued)

Name_____

Health Practices	Not Observed	Yes	No
4. Tissues are discarded once used.			
5. Children and adults cover their mouths when coughing or sneezing.			
6. Only healthy staff prepare food.			
7. Only commercially prepared canned goods are used.			
8. Foods are quickly chilled and refrigerated.			
9. Hot foods are held above 150°F.			
10. Hands are washed before preparing food and eating.			
11. Equipment and hands are thoroughly washed after working with raw meat.			
12. Cleaning pail is always washed.			
13. Flies, insects, and rodents are controlled.			
14. Foods are cooled in the refrigerator, not at room temperature.			
15. Cans with dents along side seams or with off-odors are discarded.			
16. Meats with off-odors or slimy surfaces are always thrown away.			
17. Foods are thawed only in the refrigerator.			
18. Perishable foods are prepared just prior to serving.			

■ To Review

1. Were you able to answer yes to all the statements? _____

2. If not, what could the center do to help prevent food contamination?_____

_____

_____

_____

_____

First Aid Kit

Name _____

Date _____ Period _____

■ Objectives

After completing this activity, you will be able to
- identify the items needed in a first aid kit.
- describe replacement items that are needed in a first aid kit.

■ Preparation

1. Arrange to visit a child care center.
2. Read through the first aid kit items listed below.

■ Setting

Place _____

Address _____

Telephone number _____

Contact person _____ Title _____

Date _____ Time _____ to _____

Other information _____

_____

_____

■ To Do

Check the contents of the first aid kit. If any replacements are needed, tell the director or teacher.

First Aid Kit

Quantity	Item	Complete	Replace
1	Quick reference first aid manual		
15 each	Individual adhesive bandages in ½-inch, ¾-inch, and round spot sizes		
40	Assorted individual adhesive bandages in small sizes		
10	2- by 2-inch sterile first aid dressings, individually packaged for burns and open wounds		
10	4- by 4-inch sterile first aid dressings		
1 roll	Gauze bandage, 2 inches by 5 yards		
2 rolls	Adhesive tape, 1-inch wide		
20	Disposable paper tissues		

(continued)

Quantity	Item	Complete	Replace
1 container	Mild soap for cleaning scratches and wounds.		
1 pair	Tweezers for removing splinters		
1 pair	Blunt-tipped scissors for cutting tape and bandages		
1 package	Safety pins		
1 bottle	Calamine lotion for insect bites		
5 1-ounce bottles	Syrup of ipecac		
1	Flashlight		
1	Synthetic ice pack		
1 box	Temperature strips for use on the child's forehead.		
20	Alcohol wipes		
1 package	Absorbent cotton balls		
1 bottle	Antibacterial skin cleaner		

Developing Guidance Skills

Observing Prosocial Behaviors

Activity A

Chapter 13

Name _____

Date _____ Period _____

■ Objective

After completing this activity, you will be able to
■ identify and record specific examples of prosocial behavior in young children.

■ Preparation

1. observe a group of children in an early childhood program for one hour.
2. review the examples of prosocial behavior listed below.

■ Setting

Place _____

Address _____

Telephone number _____

Contact person_____ Title _____

Date _____ Time _____ to _____

Number of children _____ Ages _____

Other information _____

_____

_____

■ To Do

Observe the group for one hour. Record specific examples of children modeling prosocial behavior.

(continued)

Prosocial Behaviors	Example Observed
1. Accepting others' feelings	
2. Verbally or physically comforting others	
3. Helping others	
4. Cooperating with others in play and cleanup time	
5. Sharing affection	
6. Showing concern	

■ To Review

1. How effective was the program you observed in reinforcing prosocial behaviors? Explain.

_____

_____

_____

_____

Child Guidance Principles

Activity B

Chapter 13

Name _____

Date _____ Period _____

■ Objective

After completing this activity, you will be able to
■ identify and record specific examples of child guidance principles.

■ Preparation

1. Observe a group of children in a classroom setting for one hour.
2. Review the guidance principles listed in the chart below.

■ Setting

Place _____

Address _____

Telephone number _____

Contact person_____ Title _____

Date _____ Time _____ to _____

Number of children _____ Ages _____ Number of adults _____

Other information _____

_____

_____

■ To Do

Observe the group for one hour. Record specific examples of teachers applying child guidance principles.

Guidance Principles	Example Observed
1. Use simple language.	
2. Speak in a relaxed voice.	
3. Be positive.	

(continued)

Name_____

Guidance Principles	Example Observed
4. Offer choices with care.	
5. Encourage independence and cooperation.	
6. Be firm.	
7. Be consistent.	
8. Provide time for change.	
9. Consider feelings.	
10. Intervene when necessary.	

Techniques for Effective Guidance

Activity C

Chapter 13

Name _____

Date _____ Period _____

■ Objective

After completing this activity, you will be able to
■ identify and record specific examples of techniques for effective guidance.

■ Preparation

1. Observe a group of children in a classroom setting for one hour.
2. Review the techniques for effective guidance listed in the chart below.

■ Setting

Place _____

Address _____

Telephone number _____

Contact person_____ Title _____

Date _____ Time _____ to _____

Number of children _____ Ages_____ Number of adults_____

Other information _____

_____

_____

■ To Do

Observe the group for one hour each day for several days. Record specific examples of teachers applying techniques for effective guidance.

Guidance Principles	Example Observed
Positive reinforcement	
Natural or artificial consequences	
Warning	

(continued)

Guidance Principles	Example Observed
Time out	
I-message	
Praising and affirming	
Suggesting	
Prompting	
Persuading	
Redirecting	
Modeling	
Active listening	
Ignoring	
Encouraging	

Evaluating Self-Concept

Activity D

Chapter 13

Name _____

Date _____ Period _____

■ Objectives

After completing this activity, you will be able to
- describe clues to a child's self-concept.
- evaluate a child's self-concept in the classroom setting.
- explain how an adult can influence a child's self-concept.

■ Preparation

1. Make arrangements to observe a child in a child care, preschool, Head Start, or kindergarten classroom.
2. Review the self-concept questions on the following chart.

■ Setting

Place _____

Address _____

Telephone number _____

Contact person _____ Title _____

Date _____ Time _____ to _____

Child's first name _____ Age _____

Other information _____

■ To Do

As you observe the child, answer the questions on the chart.

Evaluating Self-Concept	Yes	No	Sometimes
1. Does the child speak positively about himself or herself?			
2. Does the child appear to feel proud of his or her appearance?			
3. Does the child appear to be proud of his or her accomplishments?			
4. Does the child appear to accept failure?			
5. Is the child willing to try new experiences?			
6. Does the child make decisions on his or her own?			

(continued)

Name_____

Evaluating Self-Concept			
	Yes	No	Sometimes
7. Does the child appear to act independently?			
8. Does the child share his or her possessions?			
9. Is the child willing to vocalize thoughts?			
10. Does the child appear to be curious?			
11. Does the child usually appear calm and controlled?			

■ To Review

1. Do you feel this child has a good self-concept? Explain.

_____

_____

_____

_____

_____

_____

_____

_____

2. How could the classroom teacher have promoted the child's self-concept?

_____

_____

_____

_____

_____

_____

_____

_____

Guidance Problems

Possible Signs of Stress

Activity A

Chapter 14

Name _____

Date _____ **Period** _____

■ Objectives

After completing this activity, you will be able to

■ identify possible signs of stress in a group of children.
■ describe incidents in an early childhood setting that involve stressors.

■ Preparation

1. Observe a group of children in a child care setting for one hour.
2. Review the list of stressors on the next page.

■ Setting

Place _____

Address _____

Telephone number _____

Contact person_____ Title _____

Name of person observed _____

Individual's position _____

Date _____ Time _____ to _____

Number of children _____ Ages_____ Number of adults_____

Other information _____

_____

_____

■ To Do

As you observe, record the names of children and stressors you suspect. Also give detailed descriptions of each incident.

(continued)

Name_____

Stressors

accident-proneness
anger
anxiety
baby talk
bed wetting
biting
crying spells
detachment

fingernail biting
grinding teeth
hitting
indigestion
insomnia
kicking
loss of appetite
pounding heart

respiratory tract illness
stuttering
tattling
thumbsucking
upset stomach
unusual aggression
unusual laziness

Child's name	Age stressor	Description of incident

Handling Guidance Problems

Activity B

Chapter 14

Name _____

Date _____ Period _____

Objectives

After completing this activity, you will be able to
- identify incidents involving anger, fear, and overstimulation in children in a classroom setting.
- identify ways to handle children with guidance problems.

Preparation

Make arrangements to observe children in a classroom setting.

Setting

Place _____

Address _____

Telephone number _____

Contact person_____ Title _____

Name of person observed _____

Individual's position _____

Date _____ Time _____ to _____

Number of children _____ Ages_____ Number of adults _____

Other information _____

To Do

Record your observations of children with guidance problems below.

Anger

1. List two examples of how children used anger.

   A. _____

   _____

   _____

   _____

   _____

   B. _____

   _____

   _____

   _____

   _____

(continued)

2. Describe how the teacher guided each situation.

A. _____

_____

_____

_____

_____

_____

B. _____

_____

_____

_____

_____

_____

Fear

1. Describe two situations in which children experienced fear.

A. _____

_____

_____

_____

_____

_____

_____

B. _____

_____

_____

_____

_____

_____

2. Describe how the teacher guided each situation.

A. _____

_____

_____

_____

_____

(continued)

Name_____

B. _____

_____

_____

_____

_____

_____

Overstimulation

1. Describe two incidents in which disruptive behaviors were caused by overstimulation.

A. _____

_____

_____

_____

_____

_____

B. _____

_____

_____

_____

_____

_____

_____

2. Describe how the teacher guided each situation.

A. _____

_____

_____

_____

_____

_____

B. _____

_____

_____

_____

_____

_____

Establishing Classroom Rules

Observing Classroom Limits

Activity A

Chapter 15

Name _____

Date _____ Period_____

■ Objectives

After completing this activity, you will be able to
- study the classroom limits used in one setting.
- explain how the limits protected children's health and safety.

■ Preparation

1. Arrange to visit a child care center, preschool, or kindergarten.
2. Before the visit, obtain a copy of the program's classroom rules. If unavailable in written form, ask the director or teacher to share them verbally.
3. Record each rule in the chart on the next page.

■ Setting

Place _____

Address _____

Telephone number_____

Contact person_____ Title _____

Date _____ Time _____ to _____

Number of children _____ Ages_____ Number of adults_____

Other information _____

_____

_____

■ To Do

As you observe the classroom, complete the chart by writing one example of how each rule was enforced. An example is given below.

Classroom Rules	
Rule	**Teacher Behavior**
Children wipe up spills.	*Mrs. Green handed Barry a towel to wipe up the spilled milk.*

(continued)

Rule	Teacher Behavior

■ To Review

Choose three of the limits and explain how their enforcement protected the children's health and safety.

1. _____

   _____

   _____

   _____

2. _____

   _____

   _____

   _____

3. _____

   _____

   _____

   _____

Enforcing Rules

Activity B

Chapter 15

Name _____

Date _____ **Period** _____

■ Objectives

After completing this activity, you will be able to
- ■ identify ways children violate classroom rules.
- ■ describe ways classroom staff enforce rules.

■ Preparation

1. Arrange to visit a child care center, preschool, or kindergarten classroom for one hour.

■ Setting

Place _____

Address _____

Telephone number _____

Contact person_____ Title _____

Date _____ Time _____ to _____

Number of children _____ Ages_____ Number of adults_____

Other information _____

■ To Do

Observe the children and staff. Remember that all children need to develop socially responsible behavior. Complete the chart on the next page by recording examples of rules that were violated. Then record the teacher's response. Finally, record whether you agree or disagree with the response and why.

■ To Review

Based on your observations, give five guidelines for enforcing rules.

1. _____

_____

2. _____

_____

3. _____

_____

4. _____

_____

5. _____

_____

(continued)

Name_____

Name of child involved: _____

Rule violated: _____

Teacher response: _____

_____

_____

Reaction to response: _____

_____

_____

Name of child involved: _____

Rule violated: _____

Teacher response: _____

_____

_____

Reaction to response: _____

_____

_____

Name of child involved: _____

Rule violated: _____

Teacher response: _____

_____

_____

Reaction to response: _____

_____

_____

Name of child involved: _____

Rule violated: _____

Teacher response: _____

_____

_____

Reaction to response: _____

_____

_____

Handling Daily Routines

Children, Teachers, and Routines

Activity A

Chapter 16

Name _____

Date _____ **Period** _____

■ Objectives

After completing this activity, you will be able to
■ describe children's reactions to routines.
■ list ways routines are handled.

■ Preparation

Arrange to observe children in a preschool, child care, or Head Start setting. (You should discuss with the contact person a time when you are most likely to observe the routines listed.)

■ Setting

Place _____

Address _____

Telephone number _____

Contact person_____ Title _____

Date _____ Time _____ to _____

Number of children _____ Ages_____ Number of adults _____

Other information _____

_____

_____

■ To Do

Record in detail the teacher's statements and actions and the children's reactions to the following routine situations.

Routine	Teacher's Statements and Actions	Children's Reactions
Dressing and undressing		

(continued)

Routine	Teacher's Statements and Actions	Children's Reactions
Toileting		
Napping		
Eating		

■ To Review

Based on your observations, give three tips for handling routines.

1. _____

   _____

2. _____

   _____

3. _____

   _____

The Daily Schedule

Activity B

Chapter 16

Name _____

Date _____ Period _____

■ Objectives

After completing this activity, you will be able to
- ■ identify the parts of a daily schedule.
- ■ evaluate a daily schedule.
- ■ discuss the importance of alternating active and quiet activities.

■ Preparation

1. Arrange to visit a child care center, preschool, kindergarten, or Head Start program.
2. Before the observation, ask the director, principal, or teacher for a copy of the daily schedule and copy it in the space below.

■ Setting

Place _____

Address _____

Telephone number _____

Contact person _____ Title _____

Date _____ Time _____ to _____

Number of children _____ Ages _____

Other information _____

■ To Do

Evaluate the center's schedule by answering the questions that follow. Then record your observations on the effectiveness of the schedule.

The Daily Schedule

(continued)

Evaluation of Schedule

1. Are there times for the children to self-select activities? Explain.

_____

_____

_____

2. Are there small group activities? Explain.

_____

_____

_____

3. Are quiet and active activities alternated? Explain.

_____

_____

_____

4. Is cleanup time scheduled? Explain.

_____

_____

_____

5. Are there provisions for toileting and hand washing? Explain.

_____

_____

_____

6. Are there provisions for both indoor and outdoor activities? Explain.

_____

_____

_____

Observation

1. How does the written schedule compare to the actual classroom activities?

_____

_____

_____

2. How do children react to the schedule in terms of cooperation, interest, and attentiveness?

_____

_____

_____

_____

_____

Rules for Eating

Activity C

Chapter 16

Name _____

Date _____ Period _____

■ Objectives

After completing this activity, you will be able to
■ identify rules for eating.
■ describe skills the teacher used to encourage independence.

■ Preparation

1. Observe the serving of a snack, breakfast, or lunch in an early childhood program.
2. Review the rules for eating listed on the following page.

■ Setting

Place _____

Address _____

Telephone number _____

Contact person_____ Title _____

Date _____ Time _____ to _____

Type of meal _____

Other information _____

■ To Do

Describe your observations related to each of the eating rules below.

Rule	Observation
Serve small portions.	
Children should assist with serving.	
Children should assist with cleanup.	

(continued)

Rule	Observation
Children must remain at the table until everyone has finished.	
Children should wipe up their own spills.	
Children should taste all their food before pouring a second glass of milk.	

To Review

1. How effective was the program you observed in enforcing the above rules? Explain.

   _____

   _____

   _____

   _____

2. How did the teacher encourage independence as the children ate?

   _____

   _____

   _____

   _____

   _____

The Curriculum

Themes in the Classroom

Activity A

Chapter 17

Name _____

Date _____ Period _____

■ Objectives

After completing this activity, you will be able to
■ explain theme development as used by an early childhood teacher.
■ identify items and activities in a classroom related to a theme.

■ Preparation

1. Make arrangements to visit a child care center, preschool, kindergarten, or Head Start program. (Choose a time when the teacher will be able to spend about 15 minutes talking with you.)
2. Review the questions below.

■ Setting

Place _____

Address _____

Telephone number_____

Contact person_____ Title _____

Date _____ Time _____ to _____

Number of children _____ Ages _____

Other information _____

_____

■ To Do

Ask the teacher the questions below and record his or her answers. Then observe the classroom for about one hour and record examples of objects and activities that relate to the day's theme.

Questions for the teacher:

1. How do you select themes for your classroom?

_____

_____

_____

_____

(continued)

Name_____

2. How do you develop activities and materials to fit the themes?

_____

_____

_____

_____

_____

_____

3. What is the theme for today? _____

4. How long has this theme been used? _____

Objects Related to Theme	Activities Related to Theme

Learning Styles

Name _____

Date _____ Period_____

Objectives

After completing this activity, you will be able to
- ■ identify learning styles of children.
- ■ describe teaching methods that are effective with the various learning styles.

Preparation

1. Arrange to observe five children in a child care setting.
2. Before the observation, ask the teacher the names, ages, and probable learning styles of the children you will observe. Record the information below.
3. Review the text material on learning styles.

Setting

Place _____

Address _____

Telephone number _____

Contact person_____ Title _____

Date _____ Time _____ to _____

First names, ages, and probable learning styles of children:

1. _____ Age _____ Learning style _____
2. _____ Age _____ Learning style _____
3. _____ Age _____ Learning style _____
4. _____ Age _____ Learning style _____
5. _____ Age _____ Learning style _____

Other information _____

_____

_____

To Do

As you observe the children, record actions or words that indicate their learning styles. Also record methods used to effectively teach these children. Then answer the questions that follow.

Child	Signs of Learning Style	Teaching Methods

(continued)

Child	Signs of Learning Style	Teaching Methods

■ To Review

1. Do your observations confirm the teacher's evaluation of learning styles for each child? Explain.

_____

_____

_____

_____

_____

2. Were the teaching methods appropriate for each child's learning style? Explain.

_____

_____

_____

_____

Evaluating a Block Plan

Activity C

Chapter 17

Name _____

Date _____ Period _____

■ Objectives

After completing this activity, you will be able to
- review a block plan typically used in an early childhood setting.
- evaluate the completeness, practicality, and appropriateness of the block plan.

■ Preparation

1. Make arrangements to meet with a teacher or director of an early childhood program.
2. Ask the teacher or director to have a copy of a block plan available for you to take with you.
3. Review the questions below.

■ Setting

Place _____

Address _____

Telephone number _____

Contact person_____ Title _____

Date _____ Time _____ to _____

Other information _____

_____

_____

■ To Do

Examine the block plan carefully. Then ask the teacher or director the questions in Part I. Record his or her answers. Then answer the questions in Part II.

I. Teacher Planning

1. How much time did you spend working on the block plan? _____

2. How do you use the block plan during class time?

_____

_____

_____

_____

3. How does the actual class day compare with the schedule on the plan? (Are you able to fit in all activities listed? Is unplanned time left due to underplanning?)

_____

_____

_____

(continued)

4. Please clarify the following: (Include any notations or activities on the block plan you do not understand.)

_____

_____

_____

_____

II. Evaluation

1. Are all time periods throughout the day listed on the schedule? _____

2. What activities represent the following curriculum areas?

    Art:_____

    Storytelling: _____

    Socio-dramatic play and puppetry: _____

    Writing: _____

    Math: _____

    Science: _____

    Social studies: _____

    Foods: _____

    Music and movement: _____

3. Is the block plan neat and easy to read and follow? Explain.

_____

_____

4. Does the level of detail give appropriate guidance without being too complex for practical use? Explain.

_____

_____

_____

_____

_____

5. What activities fit the theme? _____

_____

_____

6. Do activities fit the developmental level of the children? Give examples.

_____

_____

_____

_____

Lesson Plans

Activity D

Chapter 17

Name _____

Date _____ Period _____

■ Objectives

After completing this activity, you will be able to
- review a teacher's lesson plan for an activity.
- observe the teacher as he or she introduces the activity.
- evaluate the effectiveness of the lesson plan in preparing the teacher for the activity.

■ Preparation

1. Make arrangements to observe a teacher in an early childhood program conducting an activity.
2. Ask the teacher for a copy of the lesson plan for the activity. Review the lesson plan at least 30 minutes before the activity. (One or two days in advance is recommended.)

■ Setting

Place _____

Address _____

Telephone number _____

Contact person_____ Title _____

Date _____ Time _____ to _____

Other information _____

_____

_____

■ To Do

As you review the lesson plan, answer the questions in Part I. After observing the activity, answer the questions in Part II.

I. Evaluation of Lesson Plan

1. Do the developmental goals explain the reason for the activity? Are they specific? Explain.

_____

_____

_____

_____

2. Are the learning objectives appropriately written? Explain.

_____

_____

_____

(continued)

Name_____

3. Is the list of materials complete? If not, what materials should be added?

_____

_____

_____

_____

4. How effective do you think the motivation will be in gaining children's attention? Explain.

_____

_____

_____

_____

5. Are procedures clear, complete, and easy to follow? If not, list any changes you would make.

_____

_____

_____

_____

_____

6. How effective do you think the closure/transition will be in ending the activity and leading the children into the next activity? Explain.

_____

_____

_____

_____

II. Observation

1. What evidence is there that the lesson plan helped prepare the teacher for the activity? Explain.

_____

_____

_____

_____

2. How did the children react to the motivation?

_____

_____

_____

_____

(continued)

3. Were children able to follow the procedures without difficulty? Explain.

_____

_____

_____

_____

4. How did the children react to the closure/transition?

_____

_____

_____

5. Did the children meet the developmental goals and learning objectives listed in the lesson plans? Explain.

_____

_____

_____

_____

6. Based on the results of the activity, what changes would you make (if any) to the lesson plan? Justify your response.

_____

_____

_____

_____

_____

Guiding Art, Blockbuilding, and Sensory Experiences

Learning Through Art Experiences

Activity A

Chapter 18

Name _____

Date _____ Period _____

■ Objective

After completing this activity, you will be able to
■ describe what children learn by participating in art experiences.

■ Preparation

1. Make arrangements to observe an art activity in a child care setting.
2. Review the learnings from art listed below.

■ Setting

Place _____

Address _____

Telephone number _____

Contact person _____ Title _____

Date _____ Time _____ to _____

Description of art activity _____

_____

_____

Other information _____

_____

_____

(continued)

■ To Do

As you observe the art activity, complete the chart by filling in the ways children learned. Record what they did or said that conveys learning.

Learning Through Art	
Learning from Art	**Observation Notes**
To express feelings	
To respect property rights of others	
To find new ways to use materials	
To use a variety of equipment and tools	
To mix materials	
To become aware of color, line, texture, and form	

(continued)

■ To Review

1. What was the most valuable learning aspect of this activity?

_____

_____

_____

_____

2. Did the children appear to enjoy this activity? Explain your response.

_____

_____

_____

_____

_____

Approaches to Painting

Name _____

Date _____ **Period** _____

■ Objective

After completing this activity, you will be able to
■ identify differences in the ways children approach painting.

■ Preparation

1. Make arrangements to observe two children painting.
2. Review the categories on the chart below.

■ Setting

Place _____

Address _____

Telephone number _____

Contact person_____ Title _____

Date _____ Time _____ to _____

Name of child 1_____ Age_____

Name of child 2_____ Age_____

Other information _____

_____

■ To Do

While observing the children, write descriptions of their behavior related to each of the categories on the chart.
Then answer the question on the next page.

Approaches to Painting		
	Child 1	**Child 2**
1. Holding brush		
2. Choice of color		

(continued)

	Child 1	Child 2
3. Dipping the brush		
4. Application of paint		
5. Use of space		

■ To Review

1. What generalizations can you make about children's use of materials? _____

_____

_____

_____

_____

_____

_____

_____

_____

_____

_____

_____

_____

_____

_____

_____

_____

Evaluating an Art Activity

Activity C

Chapter 18

Name _____

Date _____ Period _____

■ Objective

After completing this activity, you will be able to
■ evaluate an art activity, the children's responses, and the teacher's strategies.

■ Preparation

1. Make arrangements to observe an art activity in a child care setting.
2. Review the questions below.

■ Setting

Place _____

Address _____

Telephone number _____

Contact person_____ Title _____

Date _____ Time _____ to _____

Description of art activity _____

_____

_____

Other information _____

_____

_____

■ To Do

Evaluate the activity you observe by answering the questions that follow.

I. The Activity

A. Is the content worth knowing? Why or why not?

_____

_____

_____

_____

_____

(continued)

B. Was it developmentally appropriate? Explain.

_____

_____

_____

_____

_____

C. Was it interesting to the children? Explain.

_____

_____

_____

_____

D. Did the activity include opportunities for the children to test their knowledge? Explain.

_____

_____

_____

_____

II. The Children's Responses

A. Did all the children reach the objective(s)? If not, why?

_____

_____

_____

_____

_____

B. Were there behavior problems? If so, what do you think might have caused them?

_____

_____

_____

_____

_____

_____

(continued)

Name_____

III. The Teacher Strategies

A. Was the teacher well organized? Explain.

_____

_____

_____

_____

B. Did the teacher use effective teaching strategies in reaching the objectives? Give examples.

_____

_____

_____

_____

C. Did the teacher effectively introduce concepts in a stimulating manner? Give examples.

_____

_____

_____

_____

_____

_____

_____

D. Did the teacher effectively guide or manage the group? Explain.

_____

_____

_____

_____

E. Were the children involved in closure of the activity? How?

_____

_____

_____

_____

(continued)

F. What teaching strategies should be changed if this activity is repeated?

_____

_____

_____

_____

_____

_____

_____

_____

Planning an Art Activity

Activity D

Chapter 18

Name _____

Date _____ **Period** _____

■ Objectives

After completing this activity, you will be able to
- ■ plan an art activity.
- ■ develop a lesson plan for an art activity.
- ■ introduce an art activity to a group of children.
- ■ evaluate an art activity.

■ Preparation

1. Make arrangements to present an art activity at a child care center, preschool, kindergarten, or Head Start program.
2. Find out the number and ages of children with whom you will work.
3. Review the textbook material on art activities.
4. Review the sample lesson plan and evaluation in Chapter 17.
5. Think of an appropriate art activity that you could present to a group of children.

■ Setting

Place _____

Address _____

Telephone number _____

Contact person _____ Title _____

Date _____ Time _____ to _____

Number of children _____ Ages _____

Other information _____

_____

_____

■ To Do

Choose a developmentally appropriate art activity. Complete the lesson plan, Part I. After the activity, complete the evaluation of the activity, Parts II, III, and IV.

I. The Lesson Plan

Name of Activity _____

Time Scheduled _____

Classroom Area _____

(continued)

Goals (This is the purpose of the activity. What skills and knowledge will the children gain?)

Materials (What equipment and/or supplies are needed to carry out the activity?)

Introduction (This should include how the children's attention is gained. What will you say or do?)

Procedures (List what is said and done step-by-step.)

Closure (How the activity will be ended.)

(continued)

II. Evaluation of the Activity

A. Is the content worth knowing? Justify your response.

_____

_____

_____

B. Was it developmentally appropriate? Explain.

_____

_____

_____

C. Was it interesting to the children? How do you know?

_____

_____

_____

D. Did the activity include opportunities for the children to test their knowledge? Explain.

_____

_____

_____

III. The Children's Responses

A. Did all the children reach the objective(s)? If not, why?

_____

_____

_____

B. Were there behavior problems? If so, what do you think might have caused them?

_____

_____

_____

IV. The Teacher Strategies

A. Were you well organized? Explain.

_____

_____

(continued)

B. Did you use effective teaching strategies in reaching the objectives? Explain.

_____

_____

_____

C. Did you effectively introduce concepts in a stimulating manner? Explain.

_____

_____

_____

D. Did you effectively guide or manage the group? Explain.

_____

_____

_____

E. Were the children involved in closure of the activity? Explain.

_____

_____

_____

F. What teaching strategies should be changed if this activity is repeated?

_____

_____

_____

_____

_____

Blockbuilding Evaluation

Activity E

Chapter 18

Name _____

Date _____ Period _____

■ Objective

After completing this activity, you will be able to
■ describe how block play promotes learning in the four developmental domains.

■ Preparation

1. Make arrangements to observe block play in a child care setting.
2. Review the section on blockbuilding in the text.

■ Setting

Place _____

Address _____

Telephone number _____

Contact person _____ Title _____

Date _____ Time _____ to _____

Number of children _____ Ages _____

Other information _____

_____

_____

■ To Do

Observe a group of children playing with blocks for one hour. Record any specific examples of how children learn new concepts and skills observed during the hour.

Domain/Learnings	Example Observed
Physical Growth: The development and coordination of large and small muscles Hand-eye coordination skills An understanding of object-space relationship Motor coordination by lifting, carrying, and stacking	

Name_____

Domain/Learnings	Example Observed
Cognitive Growth: 　Understanding balance, weight, and measurement 　　concepts 　Exploration of shapes, sizes, and proportion 　Understanding of mathematical concepts such as *larger* 　　*than* or *smaller than* 　Understanding language concepts such as *over*, *under*, 　　*same*, *different*, and *besides* 　Experimenting with balance, gravity, and cause and effect 　Developing prediction and comparison skills 　Developing skills in sorting and classifying	
Emotional Growth: 　A sense of accomplishment and success 　The development of patience	
Social Growth: 　Cooperation skills 　Practicing sharing and taking turns 　Learning to respect the work of others	

Guiding Storytelling Experiences

Illustrations and Storytelling

Activity A

Chapter 19

Name _____

Date _____ **Period** _____

■ Objectives

After completing this activity, you will be able to
- ■ select children's books that have excellent illustrations.
- ■ identify children's reactions to illustrations.

■ Preparation

1. Make arrangements to visit a child care center, preschool, Head Start program, kindergarten, or family day care program.
2. Find out the ages of the children who will hear the stories.
3. Select three children's books for a teacher to share with the children.
4. Ask a teacher to read these three books to the children.

■ Setting

Place _____

Address _____

Telephone number _____

Contact person _____ Title _____

Date _____ Time _____ to _____

First names and ages of children:

1. _____ Age _____
2. _____ Age _____
3. _____ Age _____
4. _____ Age _____
5. _____ Age _____
6. _____ Age _____
7. _____ Age _____
8. _____ Age _____

(continued)

Other information _____

_____

_____

_____

■ To Do

Observe the children's reactions as the teacher reads the books. Complete the evaluation of the experience.

Books	Reactions of Children
Author: Illustrator: Publisher: Date of Publication:	
Author: Illustrator: Publisher: Date of Publication:	
Author: Illustrator: Publisher: Date of Publication:	

■ To Review

1. Describe the criteria you used in selecting the books.

_____

_____

_____

_____

2. Did the children react to the illustrations as you expected? Explain.

_____

_____

_____

_____

3. What have you learned in terms of choosing books with excellent illustrations?

_____

_____

_____

_____

Evaluation of a Storyteller

Activity B

Chapter 19

Name _____

Date _____ Period _____

■ Objectives

After completing this activity, you will be able to
■ evaluate the storytelling skills of a teacher.
■ explain why effective storytelling skills are important.

■ Preparation

1. Arrange to observe a storytelling session.
2. Review the evaluation criteria below.

■ Setting

Place _____

Address _____

Telephone number _____

Contact person _____ Title _____

Date _____ Time _____ to _____

Time story began _____ Time story ended _____

Number of children in group _____ Ages _____

Other information _____

_____

_____

■ To Do

Complete the chart below as the teacher tells the story. Then evaluate the storytelling session by answering the questions that follow.

The Storyteller	Yes	No
1. Chooses a book that is developmentally appropriate for the children.		
2. Uses a good introduction to establish the mood of the story.		
3. Explains unfamiliar words.		
4. Encourages child participation.		
5. Tells story with a conversational tone.		
6. Uses eye contact.		
7. Conveys enthusiasm.		

(continued)

The Storyteller

The Storyteller	Yes	No
8. Demonstrates good posture.		
9. Uses different voices for particular characters to create interest.		
10. Pronounces words clearly.		
11. Uses a lively tempo suited to children.		
12. Allows children's comments to be added to story.		
13. Makes the ending clear.		
14. Holds the book so the children can see the pictures.		

■ To Review

1. What did you observe that indicates the children were interested or disinterested in the story?

_____

_____

_____

_____

_____

2. Describe how the teacher introduced the story. Was this a positive method? Why or why not?

_____

_____

_____

_____

_____

3. Describe the relationships between the children and teacher during the activity.

_____

_____

_____

_____

_____

4. How did the teacher end the story? Was it effective? Why or why not?

_____

_____

_____

_____

_____

Evaluating a Storytelling Activity

Activity C

Chapter 19

Name _____

Date _____ Period _____

■ Objective

After completing this activity, you will be able to
■ evaluate a storytelling activity, the children's responses, and the teacher's strategies.

■ Preparation

1. Make arrangements to observe a storytelling activity in a child care setting.
2. Review the questions below.

■ Setting

Place _____

Address _____

Telephone number _____

Contact person _____ Title _____

Date _____ Time _____ to _____

Classroom area _____

Description of storytelling activity _____

_____

_____

Other information _____

_____

_____

■ To Do

Evaluate the activity you observe by answering the questions below.

I. The Activity

A. Is the content worth knowing? Why or why not?

_____

_____

_____

_____

(continued)

B. Was it developmentally appropriate? Explain.

_____

_____

_____

_____

C. Was it interesting to the children? How do you know?

_____

_____

_____

_____

D. Did the activity include opportunities for the children to test their knowledge? Explain.

_____

_____

_____

_____

II. The Children's Responses

A. Did all the children reach the objective(s)? If not, why?

_____

_____

_____

_____

_____

B. Were there behavior problems? If so, what do you think might have caused them?

_____

_____

_____

_____

_____

_____

(continued)

III. The Teacher Strategies

A. Was the teacher well organized? Explain.

_____

_____

_____

_____

B. Did the teacher use effective teaching strategies in reaching the objectives? Give examples.

_____

_____

_____

_____

_____

C. Did the teacher effectively introduce concepts in a stimulating manner? Give examples.

_____

_____

_____

_____

_____

D. Did the teacher effectively guide or manage the group? Explain.

_____

_____

_____

_____

E. Were the children involved in closure of the activity? How?

_____

_____

_____

_____

(continued)

F. What teaching strategies should be changed if this activity is repeated?

_____

_____

_____

_____

_____

_____

_____

_____

Practice Reading a Story

Activity D

Chapter 19

Name _____

Date _____ Period _____

■ Objectives

After completing this activity, you will be able to
- ■ select an appropriate storybook for young children.
- ■ read a story aloud to a small group of children.
- ■ evaluate personal storytelling skills.

■ Preparation

1. Arrange to read a story to a small group of children in a child care, preschool, Head Start, or kindergarten classroom.
2. Find out the names and ages of the children to whom you will read.
3. Select an appropriate book to read to the children.
4. Acquire a tape recorder (audio or video) to use when reading the story.

■ Setting

Place _____

Address _____

Telephone number _____

Contact person_____ Title _____

Date _____ Time _____ to _____

First names and ages of children:

1. _____ Age_____
2. _____ Age_____
3. _____ Age_____
4. _____ Age_____
5. _____ Age_____
6. _____ Age_____
7. _____ Age_____
8. _____ Age_____

Name of book _____

Author _____ Illustrator _____

Publisher _____ Date of publication _____

Time story began _____ Time story ended _____

(continued)

■ To Do

Read the story to the group of children while recording your reading. Following the storytelling experience, answer the questions below.

■ To Review

1. Describe the criteria you used in selecting the book.

   _____

   _____

   _____

   _____

   _____

   _____

2. How did you introduce the story? Was this an effective method? Why or why not?

   _____

   _____

   _____

   _____

   _____

   _____

3. What was the children's emotional response to the book?

   _____

   _____

   _____

   _____

   _____

   _____

4. Watch or listen to the recording of yourself reading the story. If you were ever to read the story again, what would you do differently?

   _____

   _____

   _____

   _____

   _____

   _____

Planning a Storytelling Activity

Activity E

Chapter 19

Name _____

Date _____ Period _____

■ Objectives

After completing this activity, you will be able to
- ■ plan a storytelling activity.
- ■ develop a lesson plan for a storytelling activity.
- ■ introduce a storytelling activity to a group of children.
- ■ evaluate a storytelling activity.

■ Preparation

1. Make arrangements to present a storytelling activity to a group of children in a child care setting.
2. Find out the number and ages of children.
3. Review the text material on achieving variety in storytelling.
4. Review the sample lesson plan and evaluation in Chapter 17.
5. Think of a storytelling activity that you could introduce to the children.

■ Setting

Place _____

Address _____

Telephone number _____

Contact person_____ Title _____

Date _____ Time _____ to _____

Number of children _____ Ages _____

Other information _____

_____

_____

■ To Do

Complete the lesson plan for the activity chosen, Part I. After the activity, complete the evaluation of the activity, Parts II, III, and IV.

I.   The Lesson Plan

Name of Activity_____

Time Scheduled_____

Classroom Area_____

(continued)

Name_____

Goals (This is the purpose of the activity. What skills and knowledge will the children gain?)

Materials (What equipment and/or supplies are needed to carry out the activity?)

Introduction (This should include how the children's attention is gained. What will you say or do?)

Procedures (List what is said and done step-by-step.)

Closure (How the activity will be ended.)

(continued)

II. Evaluation of the Activity

A. Is the content worth knowing? Justify your response.

_____

_____

_____

B. Was it developmentally appropriate? Explain.

_____

_____

_____

C. Was it interesting to the children? How do you know?

_____

_____

_____

D. Did the activity include opportunities for the children to test their knowledge? Explain.

_____

_____

_____

III. The Children's Responses

A. Did all the children reach the objective(s)? If not, why?

_____

_____

_____

_____

B. Were there behavior problems? If so, what do you think might have caused them?

_____

_____

_____

_____

IV. The Teacher Strategies

A. Were you well organized? Explain.

_____

_____

_____

(continued)

B. Did you use effective teaching strategies in reaching the objectives? Explain.

_____

_____

_____

C. Did you effectively introduce concepts in a stimulating manner? Explain.

_____

_____

_____

D. Did you effectively guide or manage the group? Explain.

_____

_____

_____

E. Were the children involved in closure of the activity? Explain.

_____

_____

_____

F. What teaching strategies should be changed if this activity is repeated?

_____

_____

_____

_____

_____

Guiding Play and Puppetry Experiences

Socio-Dramatic Play

Activity A

Chapter 20

Name _____

Date _____ **Period** _____

■ Objectives

After completing this activity, you will be able to
- ■ describe the materials and equipment used for socio-dramatic play.
- ■ discuss the role of the teacher in supporting socio-dramatic play.

■ Preparation

1. Make arrangements to observe a group of children ages three through five in a child care setting.
2. Find out the names and ages of the children you will observe.

■ Setting

Place _____

Address _____

Telephone number _____

Contact person _____ Title _____

Date _____ Time _____ to _____

First names and ages of children:

1. _____ Age _____

2. _____ Age _____

3. _____ Age _____

4. _____ Age _____

5. _____ Age_____

Other information _____

_____

_____

■ To Do

Record your observations of play in the space provided on the next page.

(continued)

Socio-Dramatic Play	
Description of area for socio-dramatic play:	
Equipment included in the dramatic play area:	
Description of play:	**Description of teacher's role:**

(continued)

■ To Review

1. Is the area for socio-dramatic play in the classroom positioned in the best location? Why or why not?

   _____

   _____

   _____

   _____

   _____

   _____

2. List six other materials that could be added to the dramatic play area.

   _____

   _____

   _____

   _____

   _____

   _____

   _____

Evaluating a Socio-Dramatic Play Activity

Activity B

Chapter 20

Name _____

Date _____ Period _____

■ Objective

After completing this activity, you will be able to
■ evaluate a socio-dramatic play activity, the children's responses, and the teacher's strategies.

■ Preparation

1. Make arrangements to observe a socio-dramatic play activity in a child care setting.
2. Review the questions below.

■ Setting

Place _____

Address _____

Telephone number _____

Contact person _____

Name of person observed _____

Date _____ Time _____ to _____

Description of socio-dramatic play activity _____

Title _____

Other information _____

_____

_____

■ To Do

Evaluate the activity you observe by answering the questions below.

I. The Activity

A. Is the content worth knowing? Why or why not?

_____

_____

_____

B. Was it developmentally appropriate? Explain.

_____

_____

_____

(continued)

C. Was it interesting to the children? Explain.

_____

_____

_____

_____

D. Did the activity include opportunities for the children to test their knowledge? Explain.

_____

_____

_____

_____

II. The Children's Responses

A. Did all the children reach the objective(s)? If not, why?

_____

_____

_____

_____

B. Were there behavior problems? If so, what do you think might have caused them?

_____

_____

_____

_____

III. The Teacher Strategies

A. Was the teacher well organized? Explain.

_____

_____

_____

_____

B. Did the teacher use effective teaching strategies in reaching the objectives? Give examples.

_____

_____

_____

_____

(continued)

C. Did the teacher effectively introduce concepts in a stimulating manner? Give examples.

_____

_____

_____

_____

D. Did the teacher effectively guide or manage the group? Explain.

_____

_____

_____

_____

E. Were the children involved in closure of the activity? How?

_____

_____

_____

_____

F. What teaching strategies should be changed if this activity is repeated?

_____

_____

_____

_____

Planning a Play or Puppetry Activity

Activity C

Chapter 20

Name _____

Date _____ Period _____

■ Objectives

After completing this activity, you will be able to
- ■ plan a play or puppetry activity.
- ■ develop a lesson plan for the activity.
- ■ introduce the activity to a group of children.
- ■ evaluate the activity.

■ Preparation

1. Make arrangements to present a play or puppetry activity in a child care setting.
2. Find out the number and ages of children with whom you will be working.
3. Review the textbook information on play and puppetry experiences.
4. Review the sample lesson plan and evaluation in Chapter 17.
5. Think of an appropriate play or puppetry activity that you could introduce to the children.

■ Setting

Place _____

Address _____

Telephone number _____

Contact person_____ Title _____

Date _____ Time _____ to _____

Number of children _____ Ages _____

Other information _____

_____

_____

■ To Do

Choose a developmentally appropriate activity. Complete the lesson plan, Part I. After the activity, complete the evaluation of the activity, Parts II, III, and IV.

I.   The Lesson Plan

Name of Activity_____

Goals (This is the purpose of the activity. What skills and knowledge will the children gain?)

(continued)

Materials (What equipment and/or supplies are needed to carry out the activity?)

Introduction (This should include how the children's attention is gained. What will you say or do?)

Procedures (List what is said and done step-by-step.)

Closure (How the activity will be ended.)

(continued)

II. Evaluation of the Activity

A. Is the content worth knowing? Justify your response.

_____

_____

_____

B. Was it developmentally appropriate? Explain.

_____

_____

_____

C. Was it interesting to the children? How do you know?

_____

_____

_____

D. Did the activity include opportunities for the children to test their knowledge? Explain.

_____

_____

_____

III. The Children's Responses

A. Did all the children reach the objective(s)? If not, why?

_____

_____

_____

B. Were there behavior problems? If so, what do you think might have caused them?

_____

_____

_____

_____

IV. The Teacher Strategies

A. Were you well organized? Explain.

_____

_____

_____

(continued)

B. Did you use effective teaching strategies in reaching the objectives? Explain.

_____

_____

_____

C. Did you effectively introduce concepts in a stimulating manner? Explain.

_____

_____

_____

D. Did you effectively guide or manage the group? Explain.

_____

_____

_____

E. Were the children involved in closure of the activity? Explain.

_____

_____

_____

F. What teaching strategies should be changed if this activity is repeated?

_____

_____

_____

_____

_____

Guiding Manuscript Writing Experiences

Children's Writing Skills

Activity A

Chapter 21

Name _____

Date _____ **Period** _____

■ Objectives

After completing this activity, you will be able to

■ identify methods of teaching writing skills in an early childhood environment.
■ list examples of a teacher's use of manuscript writing in the classroom.
■ describe differences in children's handwriting skills at four and/or five years of age.
■ discuss the teacher's role in calling attention to writing skills.

■ Preparation

Arrange to visit a child care center, preschool, Head Start, or kindergarten program.

■ Setting

Place _____

Address _____

Telephone number _____

Contact person _____ Title _____

Date _____ Time _____ to _____

Other information _____

_____

_____

■ To Do

Write responses to the following as a result of your observations.

1. List examples of the children's writing in the classroom.

_____

_____

_____

_____

_____

_____

(continued)

2. Describe the children's writing ability.

_____

_____

_____

_____

_____

_____

3. List examples of the teacher's writing in the classroom.

_____

_____

_____

_____

_____

_____

4. Why is it important that teachers have good handwriting skills?

_____

_____

_____

_____

_____

_____

5. What materials are available to encourage writing in the setting?

_____

_____

_____

_____

_____

_____

6. What additional materials could be added to encourage interest in writing?

_____

_____

_____

_____

_____

_____

(continued)

Evaluating a Handwriting Activity

Activity B

Chapter 21

Name _____

Date _____ **Period** _____

■ Objective

After completing this activity, you will be able to

■ evaluate a handwriting activity, the children's responses, and the teacher's strategies.

■ Preparation

1. Make arrangements to observe a handwriting activity in a child care setting.
2. Review the questions below.

■ Setting

Place _____

Address _____

Telephone number _____

Contact person_____ Title _____

Date _____ Time _____ to _____

Description of handwriting activity _____

_____

_____

Other information _____

_____

_____

■ To Do

Evaluate the activity you observe by answering the questions below.

I. The Activity

A. Is the content worth knowing? Why or why not?

_____

_____

_____

_____

B. Was it developmentally appropriate? Explain.

_____

_____

_____

_____

(continued)

C. Was it interesting to the children? Explain.

_____

_____

_____

_____

D. Did the activity include opportunities for the children to test their knowledge? Explain.

_____

_____

_____

_____

II. The Children's Responses

A. Did all the children reach the objective(s)? If not, why?

_____

_____

_____

_____

_____

_____

B. Were there behavior problems? If so, what do you think might have caused them?

_____

_____

_____

_____

_____

_____

III. The Teacher Strategies

A. Was the teacher well organized? Explain.

_____

_____

_____

_____

(continued)

B. Did the teacher use effective teaching strategies in reaching the objectives? Give examples.

_____

_____

_____

_____

_____

_____

C. Did the teacher effectively introduce concepts in a stimulating manner? Give examples.

_____

_____

_____

_____

_____

_____

D. Did the teacher effectively guide or manage the group? Explain.

_____

_____

_____

_____

E. Were the children involved in closure of the activity? How?

_____

_____

_____

F. What teaching strategies should be changed if this activity is repeated?

_____

_____

_____

_____

_____

Planning a Handwriting Activity

Activity C

Chapter 21

Name _____

Date _____ **Period** _____

■ Objectives

After completing this activity, you will be able to

- ■ plan a handwriting activity.
- ■ develop a lesson plan for the activity.
- ■ introduce the activity to a group of children.
- ■ evaluate the activity.

■ Preparation

1. Make arrangements to present a handwriting activity in a child care setting.
2. Find out the number and ages of children with whom you will be working.
3. Review the textbook material on techniques for encouraging writing.
4. Review the sample lesson plan and evaluation in Chapter 17.
5. Think of an appropriate handwriting activity that you could introduce to a group of children.

■ Setting

Place _____

Address _____

Telephone number _____

Contact person _____ Title _____

Date _____ Time _____ to _____

Number of children _____ Ages _____

Other information _____

_____

_____

■ To Do

Choose a developmentally appropriate activity. Complete the lesson plan, Part I. After the activity, complete the evaluation of the activity, Parts II, III, and IV.

I.   The Lesson Plan

Name of Activity _____

Time Scheduled _____

Classroom Area _____

Goals (This is the purpose of the activity. What skills and knowledge will the children gain?)

(continued)

Materials (What equipment and/or supplies are needed to carry out the activity?)

Introduction (This should include how the children's attention is gained. What will you say or do?)

Procedures (List what is said and done step-by-step.)

Closure (How the activity will be ended.)

(continued)

II. Evaluation of the Activity

A. Is the content worth knowing? Justify your response.

_____

_____

_____

B. Was it developmentally appropriate? Explain.

_____

_____

_____

C. Was it interesting to the children? How do you know?

_____

_____

_____

D. Did the activity include opportunities for the children to test their knowledge? Explain.

_____

_____

_____

III. The Children's Responses

A. Did all the children reach the objective(s)? If not, why?

_____

_____

_____

_____

B. Were there behavior problems? If so, what do you think might have caused them?

_____

_____

_____

_____

IV. The Teacher Strategies

A. Were you well organized? Explain.

_____

_____

_____

(continued)

B. Did you use effective teaching strategies in reaching the objectives? Explain.

_____

_____

_____

C. Did you effectively introduce concepts in a stimulating manner? Explain.

_____

_____

_____

D. Did you effectively guide or manage the group? Explain.

_____

_____

_____

E. Were the children involved in closure of the activity? Explain.

_____

_____

_____

F. What teaching strategies should be changed if this activity is repeated?

_____

_____

_____

_____

_____

_____

Guiding Math Experiences

Classroom Areas and Math Concepts

Activity A

Chapter 22

Name _____

Date _____ Period_____

■ Objectives

After completing this activity, you will be able to

- observe mathematical learning in the classroom.
- cite experiences in a specific classroom area that lead to the development of math concepts.
- discuss math concepts involved in a specific area of the classroom.

■ Preparation

1. Make arrangements to visit a child care, Head Start, preschool, or kindergarten program.
2. Review the text information on math concepts.

■ Setting

Place _____

Address _____

Telephone number_____

Contact person_____ Title _____

Date _____ Time _____ to _____

Number of children _____ Ages _____

Other information _____

_____

_____

■ To Do

Choose an activity area such as art, science, or music to observe. As you observe the activity area, record experiences that might lead to development of math concepts. Also record the concepts involved, such as color, shape, sets, counting, numeral identification, space, size, volume, time, and temperature.

Activity area selected _____

Experiences	Concepts Involved

(continued)

Experiences	Concepts Involved

(continued)

Mathematical Language in the Classroom

Activity B

Chapter 22

Name _____

Date _____ Period _____

■ Objectives

After completing this activity, you will be able to

■ observe for mathematical learnings in the classroom.

■ cite examples of mathematical language in children.

■ Preparation

1. Arrange to observe a child in a child care center, Head Start, preschool, or kindergarten classroom for one hour.
2. Review mathematical language in the textbook.

■ Setting

Place _____

Address _____

Telephone number _____

Contact person_____ Title _____

Date _____ Time _____ to _____

Name of child _____ Age_____

Other information _____

_____

_____

■ To Do

As you observe the child, record all examples of mathematical language.

Activity	Mathematical Language

(continued)

Activity	Mathematical Language

Math Materials and Equipment

Activity C

Chapter 22

Name _____

Date _____ Period _____

■ Objectives

After completing this activity, you will be able to

■ observe the inclusion of mathematics in the environment.

■ cite examples of equipment or materials that lead to the development of math concepts in each area of the classroom.

■ note other mathematical equipment or materials that could be included.

■ Preparation

1. Arrange to observe in a child care, Head Start, preschool, or kindergarten classroom.
2. Review information on math equipment in the textbook.

■ Setting

Place _____

Address _____

Telephone number _____

Contact person_____ Title _____

Date _____ Time _____ to _____

Number of children _____ Ages_____ Number of adults _____

Other information _____

_____

_____

■ To Do

In the space provided, list the math equipment and materials in each activity area. Give the math concepts taught by each piece of equipment. Concepts may include color, size, shape, time, temperature, space, volume, counting, numeral identification, and sets. Then list other equipment that could be added to each area to teach math concepts.

Area	Equipment Present	Concept Taught	Equipment to Add
Art			
Blockbuilding			

Name_____

Area	Equipment Present	Concept Taught	Equipment to Add
Science			
Music			
Small manipulative			
Library			
Dramatic play			
Cooking			

Evaluating a Math Activity

Activity D

Chapter 22

Name _____

Date _____ Period _____

■ Objective

After completing this activity, you will be able to

■ evaluate a math activity, the children's responses, and the teacher's strategies.

■ Preparation

1. Make arrangements to observe a math activity in a child care setting.
2. Review the questions below.

■ Setting

Place _____

Address _____

Telephone number _____

Contact person _____ Title _____

Date _____ Time _____ to _____

Description of math activity _____

_____

_____

Other information _____

_____

_____

■ To Do

Evaluate the activity you observe by answering the questions below.

I.   The Activity

A. Is the content worth knowing? Why or why not?

_____

_____

_____

_____

B. Was it developmentally appropriate? Explain.

_____

_____

_____

_____

(continued)

C. Was it interesting to the children? Explain.

_____

_____

_____

_____

D. Did the activity include opportunities for the children to test their knowledge? Explain.

_____

_____

_____

_____

II. The Children's Responses

A. Did all the children reach the objective(s)? If not, why?

_____

_____

_____

_____

_____

_____

B. Were there behavior problems? If so, what do you think might have caused them?

_____

_____

_____

_____

_____

_____

III. The Teacher Strategies

A. Was the teacher well organized? Explain.

_____

_____

_____

_____

(continued)

B. Did the teacher use effective teaching strategies in reaching the objectives? Give examples.

_____

_____

_____

_____

_____

C. Did the teacher effectively introduce concepts in a stimulating manner? Give examples.

_____

_____

_____

_____

_____

D. Did the teacher effectively guide or manage the group? Explain.

_____

_____

_____

E. Were the children involved in closure of the activity? How?

_____

_____

_____

F. What teaching strategies should be changed if this activity is repeated?

_____

_____

_____

_____

Planning a Math Activity

Activity E

Chapter 22

Name _____

Date _____ Period _____

■ Objectives

After completing this activity, you will be able to

- ■ plan a math activity.
- ■ develop a lesson plan for the activity.
- ■ introduce the activity to a group of children.
- ■ evaluate the activity.

■ Preparation

1. Make arrangements to present a math activity in a child care setting.
2. Find out the number and ages of children with whom you will be working.
3. Review the chapter material on math activities.
4. Review the sample lesson plan and evaluation in Chapter 17.
5. Think of an appropriate math activity that you could introduce to the children.

■ Setting

Place _____

Address _____

Telephone number _____

Contact person_____ Title _____

Date _____ Time _____ to _____

Number of children _____ Ages _____

Other information _____

_____

_____

■ To Do

Choose a developmentally appropriate activity. Complete the lesson plan, Part I. After the activity, complete the evaluation of the activity, Parts II, III, and IV.

I. The Lesson Plan

Name of Activity_____

Time Scheduled_____

Classroom Area_____

Goals (This is the purpose of the activity. What skills and knowledge will the children gain?)

(continued)

Introduction (This should include how the children's attention is gained. What will you say or do?)

Procedures (List what is said and done step-by-step.)

Closure (How the activity will be ended.)

Materials (What equipment and/or supplies are needed to carry out the activity?)

(continued)

II. Evaluation of the Activity

A. Is the content worth knowing? Justify your response.

_____

_____

_____

B. Was it developmentally appropriate? Explain.

_____

_____

_____

C. Was it interesting to the children? How do you know?

_____

_____

_____

D. Did the activity include opportunities for the children to test their knowledge? Explain.

_____

_____

_____

III. The Children's Responses

A. Did all the children reach the objective(s)? If not, why?

_____

_____

_____

_____

B. Were there behavior problems? If so, what do you think might have caused them?

_____

_____

_____

IV. The Teacher Strategies

A. Were you well organized? Explain.

_____

_____

_____

(continued)

B. Did you use effective teaching strategies in reaching the objectives? Explain.

_____

_____

_____

C. Did you effectively introduce concepts in a stimulating manner? Explain.

_____

_____

_____

D. Did you effectively guide or manage the group? Explain.

_____

_____

_____

E. Were the children involved in closure of the activity? Explain.

_____

_____

_____

F. What teaching strategies should be changed if this activity is repeated?

_____

_____

_____

_____

_____

Guiding Science Experiences

Science Equipment and Supplies

Activity A

Chapter 23

Name_____

Date_____ Period_____

■ Objectives

After completing this activity, you will be able to
■ identify science supplies and equipment in a classroom.
■ describe other materials that could be added to a classroom environment.

■ Preparation

1. Make arrangements to visit a child care, preschool, Head Start, or kindergarten classroom.
2. Review the checklist below.

■ Setting

Place _____

Telephone number_____

Contact person_____ Title _____

Date _____ Time _____ to _____

Number of children _____ Ages_____ Number of adults_____

Other information _____

_____

_____

■ To Do

Check off the materials listed on the following chart that are available in the classroom. Then record other equipment that could be added.

Science Supplies and Equipment

School Materials

_____ globes	_____ colored paper	_____ blocks
_____ paints	_____ scissors	_____ construction paper
_____ clay	_____ paste or glue	_____ paper cups
_____ chalk	_____ felt tip markers	_____ chart paper
_____ straws	_____ string	

(continued)

Scrap Materials

_____ discarded clocks   _____ funnels   _____ flashlights

_____ sawdust   _____ pocket mirrors   _____ airplane and
                                                                    automobile parts
_____ locks and keys   _____ large spoons

_____ metal scraps   _____ wood scraps

Classroom Pets

_____ hamsters   _____ rabbits   _____ mice

_____ harmless snakes   _____ gerbils   _____ guinea pigs

_____ frogs   _____ spiders

_____ birds   _____ fish

Construction Tools

_____ hammers   _____ saws   _____ vise

_____ rulers   _____ screwdriver   _____ pliers

Nature and Garden Items

_____ hay or straw   _____ seeds   _____ bulbs

_____ rocks or gravel   _____ growing plants   _____ garden hose

_____ bark   _____ insects   _____ flower pots

_____ nests   _____ leaves   _____ watering can

_____ garden tools   _____ shells   _____ pinecones

_____ soil and/or sand   _____ webs   _____ birdfeeder

Household Items

_____ jars   _____ pots and pans   _____ bottles

_____ strainers   _____ empty containers and trays _____ scales

_____ food coloring   _____ cardboard tubes   _____ tongs

_____ salt   _____ cloth pieces

_____ sugar   _____ measuring instruments

Gas Station Items

_____ ball bearings   _____ wheels   _____ maps

_____ jacks   _____ gears   _____ tools

Music Store Items

_____ broken string and drum heads   _____ tapes and CDs

_____ pitch pipes   _____ musical instruments   _____ tuning forks

(continued)

Medical and Dental Office Supplies

_____ corks

_____ glass tubing

_____ tongue depressors

_____ thermometers

_____ funnels

_____ microscopes

_____ models, such as teeth

Pet Store Items

_____ animals

_____ aquariums

_____ fish

_____ strainers

_____ animal cages

_____ birds

_____ butterfly nets

_____ terrariums

_____ pet food

Restaurant Items

_____ bones

_____ 5-gallon cans

_____ gallon jars

Hardware Store Supplies

_____ cement

_____ nuts and bolts

_____ sandpaper

_____ levers

_____ yardsticks

_____ flashlights

_____ nails

_____ ramps

_____ pulleys

_____ screening

_____ toy electric motors

List any other science equipment or materials that were available in the classroom for learning science.

_____

_____

_____

_____

_____

_____

List other science materials that could be added to the classroom.

_____

_____

_____

_____

_____

_____

_____

_____

(continued)

Science Literature

Name _____

Date _____ **Period** _____

■ Objectives

After completing this activity, you will be able to

review children's books for science concepts.

select a book with science concepts, prepare for reading the story, and read it to a child or several children.

record conversation that occurs during the experience.

■ Preparation

1. Visit a library and check out three children's books that contain science concepts.
2. List the books, authors, and science concepts in the space provided.
3. Make arrangements to read one book to a child or small group of children.
4. Record the names and ages of the children to whom you will read.
5. Choose an appropriate book from the three and prepare to read the story to the children by reading it aloud in front of a mirror.

■ Setting

Place _____

Address _____

Telephone number _____

Contact person_____ Title _____

Date _____ Time _____ to _____

Names and ages of children:

1. _____ Age_____

2. _____ Age_____

3. _____ Age_____

4. _____ Age_____

5. _____ Age_____

6. _____ Age_____

Other information _____

_____

_____

■ To Do

Read your chosen story to the children. Then answer the questions that follow.

(continued)

Guiding Science Experiences   221

Name and Author of Book	Science Concepts
1.	
2.	
3.	

To Review

1. How did you decide which of the three books you would read?

_____

_____

_____

_____

2. How did you introduce the book?

_____

_____

_____

_____

3. What were the children's responses to the book?

_____

_____

_____

_____

(continued)

4. What conversation occurred during the activity that showed evidence of children learning science concepts?

_____

_____

_____

_____

_____

5. How did you end the activity?

_____

_____

_____

_____

6. Do you think you chose the right story? Why or why not?

_____

_____

_____

_____

Evaluating a Science Activity

Activity C

Chapter 23

Name _____

Date _____ Period _____

■ Objective

After completing this activity, you will be able to
■ evaluate a science activity, the children's responses, and the teacher's strategies.

■ Preparation

1. Make arrangements to observe a science activity in a child care setting.
2. Review the questions below.

■ Setting

Place _____

Address _____

Telephone number _____

Contact person _____ Title _____

Date _____ Time _____ to _____

Description of science activity _____

_____

_____

Other information _____

_____

_____

■ To Do

Evaluate the activity you observe by answering the questions below.

I. The Activity

A. Is the content worth knowing? Why or why not?

_____

_____

_____

_____

B. Was it developmentally appropriate? Explain.

_____

_____

_____

_____

(continued)

C. Was it interesting to the children? Explain.

_____

_____

_____

_____

D. Did the activity include opportunities for the children to test their knowledge? Explain.

_____

_____

_____

_____

II. The Children's Responses

A. Did all the children reach the objective(s)? If not, why?

_____

_____

_____

_____

_____

_____

B. Were there behavior problems? If so, what do you think might have caused them?

_____

_____

_____

_____

_____

_____

III. The Teacher Strategies

A. Was the teacher well organized? Explain.

_____

_____

_____

_____

(continued)

B. Did the teacher use effective teaching strategies in reaching the objectives? Give examples.

_____

_____

_____

_____

_____

_____

C. Did the teacher effectively introduce concepts in a stimulating manner? Give examples.

_____

_____

_____

_____

_____

_____

D. Did the teacher effectively guide or manage the group? Explain.

_____

_____

_____

_____

E. Were the children involved in closure of the activity? How?

_____

_____

_____

_____

F. What teaching strategies should be changed if this activity is repeated?

_____

_____

_____

_____

_____

_____

Planning a Science Activity

Activity D

Chapter 23

Name _____

Date _____ Period_____

■ Objectives

After completing this activity, you will be able to
- ■ plan a science activity.
- ■ develop a lesson plan for the activity.
- ■ introduce the activity to a group of children.
- ■ evaluate the activity.

■ Preparation

1. Make arrangements to present a science activity in a child care setting.
2. Find out the number and ages of children with whom you will be working.
3. Review the chapter material on science activities.
4. Review the sample lesson plan and evaluation in Chapter 17.
5. Think of an appropriate science activity you could introduce to the children.

■ Setting

Place _____

Address _____

Telephone number _____

Contact person_____ Title _____

Date _____ Time _____ to _____

Number of children _____ Ages _____

Other information _____

_____

_____

■ To Do

Choose a developmentally appropriate activity. Complete the lesson plan, Part I. After the activity, complete the evaluation of the activity, Parts II, III, and IV.

I.   The Lesson Plan

Name of Activity_____

Time Scheduled_____

Classroom Area_____

Goals (This is the purpose of the activity. What skills and knowledge will the children gain?)

(continued)

Materials (What equipment and/or supplies are needed to carry out the activity?)

Introduction (This should include how the children's attention is gained. What will you say or do?)

Procedures (List what is said and done step-by-step.)

Closure (How the activity will be ended.)

(continued)

II. Evaluation of the Activity

A. Is the content worth knowing? Justify your response.

_____

_____

_____

B. Was it developmentally appropriate? Explain.

_____

_____

_____

C. Was it interesting to the children? How do you know?

_____

_____

_____

D. Did the activity include opportunities for the children to test their knowledge? Explain.

_____

_____

_____

III. The Children's Responses

A. Did all the children reach the objective(s)? If not, why?

_____

_____

_____

_____

B. Were there behavior problems? If so, what do you think might have caused them?

_____

_____

_____

_____

IV. The Teacher Strategies

A. Were you well organized? Explain.

_____

_____

_____

(continued)

B. Did you use effective teaching strategies in reaching the objectives? Explain.

_____

_____

_____

C. Did you effectively introduce concepts in a stimulating manner? Explain.

_____

_____

_____

D. Did you effectively guide or manage the group? Explain.

_____

_____

_____

E. Were the children involved in closure of the activity? Explain.

_____

_____

_____

F. What teaching strategies should be changed if this activity is repeated?

_____

_____

_____

_____

Guiding Social Studies Experiences

Evaluating a Social Studies Activity

Activity A

Chapter 24

Name _____

Date _____ Period _____

■ Objective

After completing this activity, you will be able to

■ evaluate a social studies activity, the children's responses, and the teacher's strategies.

■ Preparation

1. Make arrangements to observe a social studies activity in a child care setting.
2. Review the questions below.

■ Setting

Place _____

Address _____

Telephone number _____

Contact person_____ Title _____

Date _____ Time _____ to _____

Description of social studies activity _____

_____

_____

Other information _____

_____

_____

■ To Do

Evaluate the activity you observe by answering the questions below.

I. The Activity

A. Is the content worth knowing? Why or why not?

_____

_____

_____

_____

(continued)

B. Was it developmentally appropriate? Explain.

_____

_____

_____

_____

C. Was it interesting to the children? Explain.

_____

_____

_____

_____

D. Did the activity include opportunities for the children to test their knowledge? Explain.

_____

_____

_____

_____

II. The Children's Responses

A. Did all the children reach the objective(s)? If not, why?

_____

_____

_____

_____

_____

_____

B. Were there behavior problems? If so, what do you think may have caused them?

_____

_____

_____

_____

_____

_____

(continued)

III. The Teacher Strategies

A. Was the teacher well organized? Explain.

_____

_____

_____

_____

B. Did the teacher use effective teaching strategies in reaching the objectives? Give examples.

_____

_____

_____

_____

_____

_____

_____

_____

C. Did the teacher effectively introduce concepts in a stimulating manner? Give examples.

_____

_____

_____

_____

_____

_____

_____

D. Did the teacher effectively guide or manage the group? Explain.

_____

_____

_____

_____

E. Were the children involved in closure of the activity? How?

_____

_____

_____

(continued)

F. What teaching strategies should be changed if this activity is repeated?

_____

_____

_____

_____

_____

_____

_____

_____

Planning a Social Studies Activity

Activity B

Chapter 24

Name _____

Date _____ Period _____

■ Objectives

After completing this activity, you will be able to

- ■ plan a social studies activity.
- ■ develop a lesson plan for the activity.
- ■ introduce the activity to a group of children.
- ■ evaluate the activity.

■ Preparation

1. Make arrangements to present a social studies activity in a child care setting.
2. Find out the number and ages of children with whom you will be working.
3. Review the chapter material on social studies activities.
4. Review the sample lesson plan and evaluation in Chapter 17.
5. Think of an appropriate social studies activity that you could introduce to the children.

■ Setting

Place _____

Address _____

Telephone number _____

Contact person _____ Title _____

Date _____ Time _____ to _____

Number of children _____ Ages _____

Other information _____

_____

_____

■ To Do

Choose a developmentally appropriate activity. Complete the lesson plan, Part I. After the activity, complete the evaluation of the activity, Part II, III, and IV.

I. The Lesson Plan

Name of Activity _____

Time Scheduled _____

Classroom Area _____

Goals (This is the purpose of the activity. What skills and knowledge will the children gain?)

(continued)

Materials (What equipment and/or supplies are needed to carry out the activity?)

Introduction (This should include how the children's attention is gained. What will you say or do?)

Procedures (List what is said and done step-by-step.)

Closure (How the activity will be ended.)

(continued)

II. Evaluation of the Activity

A. Is the content worth knowing? Justify your response.

_____

_____

_____

B. Was it developmentally appropriate? Explain.

_____

_____

_____

C. Was it interesting to the children? How do you know?

_____

_____

_____

D. Did the activity include opportunities for the children to test their knowledge? Explain.

_____

_____

_____

III. The Children's Responses

A. Did all the children reach the objective(s)? If not, why?

_____

_____

_____

B. Were there behavior problems? If so, what do you think might have caused them?

_____

_____

_____

IV. The Teacher Strategies

A. Were you well organized? Explain.

_____

_____

(continued)

B. Did you use effective teaching strategies in reaching the objectives? Explain.

_____

_____

_____

C. Did you effectively introduce concepts in a stimulating manner? Explain.

_____

_____

_____

D. Did you effectively guide or manage the group? Explain.

_____

_____

_____

E. Were the children involved in closure of the activity? Explain.

_____

_____

_____

F. What teaching strategies should be changed if this activity is repeated?

_____

_____

_____

_____

Guiding Food and Nutrition Experiences

Important Food Learnings

Activity A

Chapter 25

Name _____

Date _____ Period_____

■ Objectives

After completing this activity, you will be able to

■ cite examples of important learnings during a classroom cooking activity.

■ evaluate the cooking activity.

■ Preparation

1. Make arrangements to observe a cooking activity in a preschool, child care, Head Start, or kindergarten program.
2. Review the important learnings in the chart below.

Setting

Place _____

Address _____

Telephone number_____

Contact person_____ Title _____

Date _____ Time _____ to _____

Number of children participating _____ Ages _____

Other information _____

_____

_____

■ To Do

As you observe, record teacher actions or words that teach each concept in the chart. Then write the children's reactions to each teaching.

Important Learnings	Caregiver Actions or Words	Children's Reactions to Teaching
Understanding cleanliness and safety measures		

(continued)

Name_____

Important Learnings	Caregiver Actions or Words	Children's Reactions to Teaching
Following directions		
Understanding nutrition guidelines		
Using motor skills		
Understanding food sources		
Identifying foods in the Food Guide Pyramid for Young Children		
Using all senses		
Counting and measuring carefully		
Understanding basic chemical changes		
Understanding the use of cooking equipment		
Understanding cooking processes		

(continued)

Evaluating a Cooking Activity

Activity B

Chapter 25

Name _____

Date _____ Period _____

■ Objective

After completing this activity, you will be able to

■ evaluate a cooking activity, the children's responses, and the teacher's strategies.

■ Preparation

1. Make arrangements to visit a cooking activity in a child care center.
2. Review the questions below.

■ Setting

Place _____

Address _____

Telephone number _____

Contact person _____ Title _____

Date _____ Time _____ to _____

Description of cooking activity _____

_____

_____

Other information _____

_____

_____

■ To Do

Evaluate the activity you observe by answering the questions below.

I. The Activity

A. Is the content worth knowing? Why or why not?

_____

_____

_____

_____

B. Was it developmentally appropriate? Explain.

_____

_____

_____

_____

(continued)

C. Was it interesting to the children? Explain.

_____

_____

_____

_____

D. Did the activity include opportunities for the children to test their knowledge? Explain.

_____

_____

_____

_____

II. The Children's Responses

A. Did all the children reach the objective(s)? If not, why?

_____

_____

_____

_____

_____

_____

B. Were there behavior problems? If so, what do you think might have caused them?

_____

_____

_____

_____

_____

III. The Teacher Strategies

A. Was the teacher well organized? Explain.

_____

_____

_____

_____

(continued)

B. Did the teacher use effective teaching strategies in reaching the objectives? Give examples.

_____

_____

_____

_____

_____

_____

C. Did the teacher effectively introduce concepts in a stimulating manner? Give examples.

_____

_____

_____

_____

_____

_____

D. Did the teacher effectively guide or manage the group? Explain.

_____

_____

_____

E. Were the children involved in closure of the activity? How?

_____

_____

_____

F. What teaching strategies should be changed if this activity is repeated?

_____

_____

_____

_____

_____

Evaluating Children's Learnings

Activity C

Chapter 25

Name _____

Date _____ Period _____

■ Objectives

After completing this activity, you will be able to

- ■ plan a classroom cooking activity.
- ■ list the supplies, including ingredients and utensils, that will be needed for the activity.
- ■ evaluate what the children learned.

■ Preparation

1. Make arrangements to conduct a cooking activity in a child care setting.
2. Find out the number and ages of children with whom you will work.
3. Review the questions below.
4. Select a recipe to use in the activity and list the ingredients and supplies needed below.

■ Setting

Place _____

Address _____

Telephone number _____

Contact person_____ Title _____

Date _____ Time _____ to _____

Number of children in group _____ Ages _____

Other information _____

_____

_____

■ To Do

Before conducting the cooking activity, answer Part A of each question. Complete Part B after conducting the activity.

1. A: Describe the activity you intend to introduce.

_____

_____

_____

_____

_____

_____

_____

_____

(continued)

2. A: Include uses of all the senses. What will you say or demonstrate?

_____

_____

_____

_____

_____

B: Evaluation of participants' learning.

_____

_____

_____

_____

_____

3. A: Include careful counting and measuring. What will you say or demonstrate?

_____

_____

_____

_____

_____

B: Evaluation of participants' learning.

_____

_____

_____

_____

_____

4. A: Include the understanding of basic chemical changes. What will you say or demonstrate?

_____

_____

_____

_____

B: Evaluation of participants' learning.

_____

_____

_____

_____

(continued)

5. A: Include the use of motor skills. What will you say or demonstrate?

_____

_____

_____

B: Evaluation of participants' learning.

_____

_____

_____

_____

6. A: Include the names of food and the Food Guide Pyramid for Young Children. What will you say or demonstrate?

_____

_____

_____

_____

B: Evaluation of participants' learning.

_____

_____

_____

_____

7. A: Include the understanding of cooking equipment and cooking process. What will you say or demonstrate?

_____

_____

_____

_____

B: Evaluation of participants' learning.

_____

_____

_____

Planning a Food Activity

Name _____

Date _____ Period _____

■ Objectives

After completing this activity, you will be able to

- ■ plan a food activity.
- ■ develop a lesson plan for the activity.
- ■ introduce the activity to a group of children.
- ■ evaluate the activity.

■ Preparation

1. Make arrangements to present a food activity in a child care setting.
2. Find out the number and ages of children with whom you will work.
3. Review the chapter material on science activities.
4. Review the sample lesson plan and evaluation in Chapter 17.
5. Think of an appropriate food activity that you could introduce to the children.

■ Setting

Place _____

Address _____

Telephone number _____

Contact person_____ Title _____

Date _____ Time _____ to _____

Number of children _____ Ages _____

Other information _____

_____

_____

■ To Do

Choose a developmentally appropriate activity. Complete the lesson plan, Part I. After the activity, complete the evaluation of the activity, Parts II, III, and IV.

I.   The Lesson Plan

Name of Activity_____

Time Scheduled_____

Classroom Area_____

Goals (This is the purpose of the activity. What skills and knowledge will the children gain?)

(continued)

Materials (What equipment and/or supplies are needed to carry out the activity?)

Introduction (This should include how the children's attention is gained. What will you say or do?)

Procedures (List what is said and done step-by-step.)

Closure (How the activity will be ended.)

(continued)

II. Evaluation of the Activity

A. Is the content worth knowing? Justify your response.

_____

_____

_____

B. Was it developmentally appropriate? Explain.

_____

_____

_____

C. Was it interesting to the children? How do you know?

_____

_____

_____

D. Did the activity include opportunities for the children to test their knowledge? Explain.

_____

_____

_____

II. The Children's Responses

A. Did all the children reach the objective(s)? If not, why?

_____

_____

_____

B. Were there behavior problems? If so, what do you think might have caused them?

_____

_____

_____

IV. The Teacher Strategies

A. Were you well organized? Explain.

_____

_____

_____

(continued)

B. Did you use effective teaching strategies in reaching the objectives? Explain.

_____

_____

_____

C. Did you effectively introduce concepts in a stimulating manner? Explain.

_____

_____

_____

D. Did you effectively guide or manage the group? Explain.

_____

_____

_____

E. Were the children involved in closure of the activity? Explain.

_____

_____

_____

F. What teaching strategies should be changed if this activity is repeated?

_____

_____

_____

_____

_____

_____

Observing Snack Time

Name _____

Date _____ Period _____

■ Objectives

After completing this activity, you will be able to

■ describe snack time at a child care center.

■ discuss the importance of snack time.

■ Preparation

1. Make arrangements to visit a preschool, child care center, kindergarten, Head Start program, or family child care program to observe snack time.
2. Review the questions below.

■ Setting

Place _____

Address _____

Telephone number _____

Contact person _____ Title _____

Date _____ Time _____ to _____

Type of snack served _____

Number of children _____ Ages _____

Other information _____

_____

_____

■ To Do

As you observe, answer the questions below.

1. Describe the snack that was served.

_____

_____

_____

_____

_____

2. Describe where the snack was served.

_____

_____

_____

_____

(continued)

Name_____

3. Who served the snack?

_____

_____

4. Were there any problems? If so, how were they solved?

_____

_____

_____

_____

_____

_____

5. How could the problems have been prevented?

_____

_____

_____

_____

_____

_____

■ To Review

1. Discuss the benefits of having a snack time.

_____

_____

_____

_____

_____

_____

Guiding Music and Movement Experiences

Music Experiences

Activity A

Chapter 26

Name _____

Date _____ Period _____

■ Objectives

After completing this activity, you will be able to

■ describe a music experience.

■ describe the teacher's role in the music experience.

■ Preparation

Make arrangements to observe a music activity at a child care, Head Start, or kindergarten program.

■ Setting

Place _____

Address _____

Telephone number _____

Contact person_____ Title _____

Date _____ Time _____ to _____

Number of children _____ Ages_____ Number of adults _____

Equipment used (if any) _____

Other information _____

_____

_____

■ To Do

In the space provided, describe in detail the words and actions that take place during the activity. Also describe the teacher's role in the activity.

Words and Actions During the Activity	Description of Teacher's Role

(continued)

Name_____

Words and Actions During the Activity	Description of Teacher's Role

Creating a Song

Activity B

Chapter 26

Name _____

Date _____ Period _____

■ Objectives

After completing this activity, you will be able to

- ■ create a song using a familiar melody and adding new words.
- ■ introduce the song to a small group of children.
- ■ evaluate the experience.

■ Preparation

Make arrangements to teach a song to a group of children in a child care, preschool, kindergarten, or Head Start program.

■ Setting

Place _____

Address _____

Telephone number _____

Contact person_____ Title _____

Date _____ Time _____ to _____

First names and ages of children participating:

1. _____ Age_____

2. _____ Age_____

3. _____ Age_____

4. _____ Age_____

5. _____ Age_____

6. _____ Age_____

Other information _____

_____

_____

■ To Do

Create a song using a familiar melody such as "Twinkle, Twinkle Little Star" or "Mary Had a Little Lamb." Write the name of the melody and the words below. Introduce the song to a small group of children. Describe the children's reactions to the experience and evaluate your presentation skills.

Melody _____

Words for song:

(continued)

Words for song (cont.):

■ To Review

1. Describe exactly what happened during the activity.

_____

_____

_____

_____

_____

_____

_____

_____

_____

_____

2. Describe your personal reaction to the activity.

_____

_____

_____

_____

_____

_____

_____

_____

_____

_____

Evaluating a Music Activity

Activity C

Chapter 26

Name _____

Date _____ **Period** _____

■ Objective

After completing this activity, you will be able to

■ evaluate a music activity, the children's responses, and the teacher's strategies.

■ Preparation

1. Make arrangements to observe a music activity in a child care setting.
2. Review the questions below.

■ Setting

Place _____

Address _____

Telephone number _____

Contact person_____ Title _____

Date _____ Time _____ to _____

Description of music activity _____

_____

_____

Other information _____

_____

_____

■ To Do

Evaluate the activity you observe by answering the questions below.

I.   The Activity

A. Is the content worth knowing? Why or why not?

_____

_____

_____

_____

B. Was it developmentally appropriate? Explain.

_____

_____

_____

(continued)

C. Was it interesting to the children? Explain.

_____

_____

_____

D. Did the activity include opportunities for the children to test their knowledge? Explain.

_____

_____

_____

II. The Children's Responses

A. Did all the children reach the objective(s)? If not, why?

_____

_____

_____

_____

_____

_____

B. Were there behavior problems? If so, what do you think might have caused them?

_____

_____

_____

_____

_____

_____

III. The Teacher Strategies

A. Was the teacher well organized? Explain.

_____

_____

_____

_____

(continued)

B. Did the teacher use effective teaching strategies in reaching the objectives? Give examples.

_____

_____

_____

_____

_____

_____

C. Did the teacher effectively introduce concepts in a stimulating manner? Give examples.

_____

_____

_____

_____

_____

_____

D. Did the teacher effectively guide or manage the group? Explain.

_____

_____

_____

E. Were the children involved in closure of the activity? How?

_____

_____

_____

F. What teaching strategies should be changed if this activity is repeated?

_____

_____

_____

_____

_____

Expression of Feelings Through Movement

Activity D

Chapter 26

Name _____

Date _____ Period _____

■ Objectives

After completing this activity, you will be able to

- observe a movement experience.
- describe the feelings and ideas expressed by the children during the activity.

■ Preparation

Make arrangements to observe a movement activity at a child care, preschool, Head Start, or kindergarten program.

■ Setting

Place _____

Address _____

Telephone number _____

Contact person _____ Title _____

Date _____ Time _____ to _____

Number of children _____ Ages _____ Number of adults _____

Other information _____

_____

_____

■ To Do

As you observe, describe the feelings and ideas expressed by the children in the space provided.

Child's Name	Movement	Feelings	Ideas

(continued)

Child's Name	Movement	Feelings	Ideas

Planning a Music or Movement Activity

Activity E

Chapter 26

Name _____

Date _____ Period _____

■ Objectives

After completing this activity, you will be able to

- ■ plan a music or movement activity.
- ■ develop a lesson plan for the activity.
- ■ introduce the activity to a group of children.
- ■ evaluate the activity.

■ Preparation

1. Make arrangements to present a music or movement activity at a child care center, preschool, kindergarten, or Head Start program.
2. Find out the number and ages of children with whom you will work.
3. Review the chapter material on music and movement activities.
4. Review the sample lesson plan and evaluation in Chapter 17.
5. Think of an appropriate music activity that you could introduce to the children.

■ Setting

Place _____

Address _____

Telephone number _____

Contact person_____ Title _____

Date _____ Time _____ to _____

Number of children _____ Ages_____ Number of adults _____

Other information _____

_____

_____

■ To Do

Choose a developmentally appropriate activity. Complete the lesson plan, Part I. After the activity, complete the evaluation of the activity, Parts II, III, and IV.

I.   The Lesson Plan

Name of Activity_____

Time Scheduled_____

Classroom Area_____

Goals (This is the purpose of the activity. What skills and knowledge will the children gain?)

(continued)

Materials (What equipment and/or supplies are needed to carry out the activity?)

Introduction (This should include how the children's attention is gained. What will you say or do?)

Procedures (List what is said and done step-by-step.)

Closure (How the activity will be ended.)

(continued)

II. Evaluation of the Activity

A. Is the content worth knowing? Justify your response.

_____

_____

_____

B. Was it developmentally appropriate? Explain.

_____

_____

_____

C. Was it interesting to the children? How do you know?

_____

_____

_____

D. Did the activity include opportunities for the children to test their knowledge? Explain.

_____

_____

_____

III. The Children's Responses

A. Did all the children reach the objective(s)? If not, why?

_____

_____

_____

_____

B. Were there behavior problems? If so, what do you think might have caused them?

_____

_____

_____

_____

IV. The Teacher Strategies

A. Were you well organized? Explain.

_____

_____

(continued)

B. Did you use effective teaching strategies in reaching the objectives? Explain.

_____

_____

_____

C. Did you effectively introduce concepts in a stimulating manner? Explain.

_____

_____

_____

D. Did you effectively guide or manage the group? Explain.

_____

_____

_____

E. Were the children involved in closure of the activity? Explain.

_____

_____

_____

F. What teaching strategies should be changed if this activity is repeated?

_____

_____

_____

_____

_____

Guiding Field Trip Experiences

The Pretrip

Activity A

Chapter 27

Name _____

Date _____ Period _____

■ Objectives

After completing this activity, you will be able to

■ select a field trip site for a group of children.

■ take a pretrip to the site.

■ Preparation

1. Choose a field trip site that you think would be worthwhile for a group of children to visit.
2. Make arrangements to make a pretrip visit to the site.
3. Review the questions in the form below.

■ Setting

Site _____

Address _____

Telephone number _____

Contact person_____ Title _____

Date _____ Time _____ to _____

Other information _____

_____

_____

■ To Do

Evaluate the field trip site using the form below.

I. Communicating to the Resource Person

1. Describe to the person the goals you expect to reach. Record the conversation.

_____

_____

_____

_____

_____

_____

(continued)

2. Describe the developmental level of the children to the person. Record the conversation.

_____

_____

_____

_____

3. Describe the children's interests to the person. Record the conversation.

_____

_____

_____

_____

_____

_____

4. Describe to the person the types of questions the children may ask. Record the conversation.

_____

_____

_____

_____

_____

_____

_____

_____

_____

II. Preparing Yourself

1. Where are the bathrooms located?

_____

_____

2. If a bus is used, where is parking located?

_____

_____

3. What special learning opportunities did you observe?

_____

_____

_____

_____

_____

(continued)

Name_____

III. Evaluating the Site

1. Are there any dangers involved? Support your response.

_____

_____

_____

_____

_____

2. Would the experience be valuable for the children? Explain.

_____

_____

_____

_____

_____

3. If costs are involved, is the trip the best use of your resources? Why or why not?

_____

_____

_____

_____

4. At what time of the day would it be best to schedule a trip to this site? Why?

_____

_____

_____

Evaluating a Field Trip

Activity B

Chapter 27

Name _____

Date _____ Period _____

■ Objective

After completing this activity, you will be able to

■ evaluate a field trip, the children's responses, and the teacher's strategies.

■ Preparation

1. Make arrangements to go on a field trip with children from a child care center, preschool, kindergarten, or Head Start program.
2. Review the questions below.

■ Setting

Site _____

Address _____

Telephone number _____

Contact person _____ Title _____

Date _____ Time _____ to _____

Description of field trip _____

_____

_____

Other information _____

_____

_____

■ To Do

Evaluate the activity you observe by answering the questions below.

I.   The Activity

A. Is the content worth knowing? Why or why not?

_____

_____

_____

_____

B. Was it developmentally appropriate? Explain.

_____

_____

_____

_____

(continued)

C. Was it interesting to the children? Explain.

_____

_____

_____

_____

D. Did the activity include opportunities for the children to test their knowledge? Explain.

_____

_____

_____

_____

II. The Children's Responses

A. Did all the children reach the objective(s)? If not, why?

_____

_____

_____

_____

_____

_____

B. Were there behavior problems? If so, what do you think might have caused them?

_____

_____

_____

_____

_____

_____

III. The Teacher Strategies

A. Was the teacher well organized? Explain.

_____

_____

_____

_____

(continued)

B. Did the teacher use effective teaching strategies in reaching the objectives? Give examples.

_____

_____

_____

_____

_____

_____

C. Did the teacher effectively introduce concepts in a stimulating manner? Give examples.

_____

_____

_____

_____

_____

_____

D. Did the teacher effectively guide or manage the group? Explain.

_____

_____

_____

_____

E. Were the children involved in closure of the activity? How?

_____

_____

_____

_____

F. What teaching strategies should be changed if this activity is repeated?

_____

_____

_____

_____

_____

Planning a Field Trip

Name _____

Date _____ Period _____

■ Objectives

After completing this activity, you will be able to

■ plan a field trip.
■ develop a lesson plan for the trip.
■ take a group of children on the field trip.
■ evaluate the field trip.

■ Preparation

1. Make arrangements to take a group of children from a child care center, preschool, kindergarten, or Head Start program on a field trip with the teacher's supervision.
2. Find out the number and ages of children with whom you will work.
3. Review the chapter material on planning a field trip.
4. Review the sample lesson plan and evaluation in Chapter 17.
5. Think of a field trip that is appropriate for the children.

■ Setting

Child care program _____

Address _____

Telephone number _____

Contact person _____ Title _____

Date _____ Time _____ to _____

Number of children _____ Ages _____

Field trip location _____

Address _____

Telephone number _____

Contact person _____ Title _____

Other information _____

_____

_____

■ To Do

Choose a developmentally appropriate field trip. Complete the lesson plan, Part I. After the activity, complete the evaluation of the activity, Parts II, III, and IV.

I. The Lesson Plan

Name of Activity _____

Time Scheduled _____

Classroom Area _____

(continued)

Goals (This is the purpose of the activity. What skills and knowledge will the children gain?)

Materials (What equipment and/or supplies are needed to carry out the activity?)

Introduction (This should include how the children's attention is gained. What will you say or do?)

Procedures (List what is said and done step-by-step.)

Closure (How the activity will be ended.)

(continued)

II. Evaluation of the Activity

A. Is the content worth knowing? Justify your response.

_____

_____

_____

B. Was it developmentally appropriate? Explain.

_____

_____

_____

C. Was it interesting to the children? How do you know?

_____

_____

_____

D. Did the activity include opportunities for the children to test their knowledge? Explain.

_____

_____

_____

III. The Children's Responses

A. Did all the children reach the objective(s)? If not, why?

_____

_____

_____

_____

B. Were there behavior problems? If so, what do you think might have caused them?

_____

_____

_____

_____

IV. The Teacher Strategies

A. Were you well organized? Explain.

_____

_____

_____

(continued)

B. Did you use effective teaching strategies in reaching the objectives? Explain.

_____

_____

_____

C. Did you effectively introduce concepts in a stimulating manner? Explain.

_____

_____

_____

D. Did you effectively guide or manage the group? Explain.

_____

_____

_____

E. Were the children involved in closure of the activity? Explain.

_____

_____

_____

F. What teaching strategies should be changed if this activity is repeated?

_____

_____

_____

_____

_____

Programs for Infants and Toddlers

Toddler Environment

Activity A

Chapter 28

Name _____

Date _____ Period_____

■ Objectives

After completing this activity, you will be able to

■ sketch the room arrangement for a toddler program on graph paper.

■ evaluate the use of space in the room.

■ Preparation

1. Make arrangements to visit a child care center with a toddler program.
2. Read the chapter information on infant and toddler environments.
3. You will need a ruler and pencil to draw the floor plan.

■ Setting

Place _____

Address _____

Telephone number_____

Contact person_____ Title _____

Date _____ Time _____ to _____

Number of children _____ Ages_____ Number of adults_____

Other information _____

■ To Do

Sketch the room arrangement on the graph paper provided. Then evaluate the arrangement by answering the questions that follow.

(continued)

Name_____

Room Arrangement

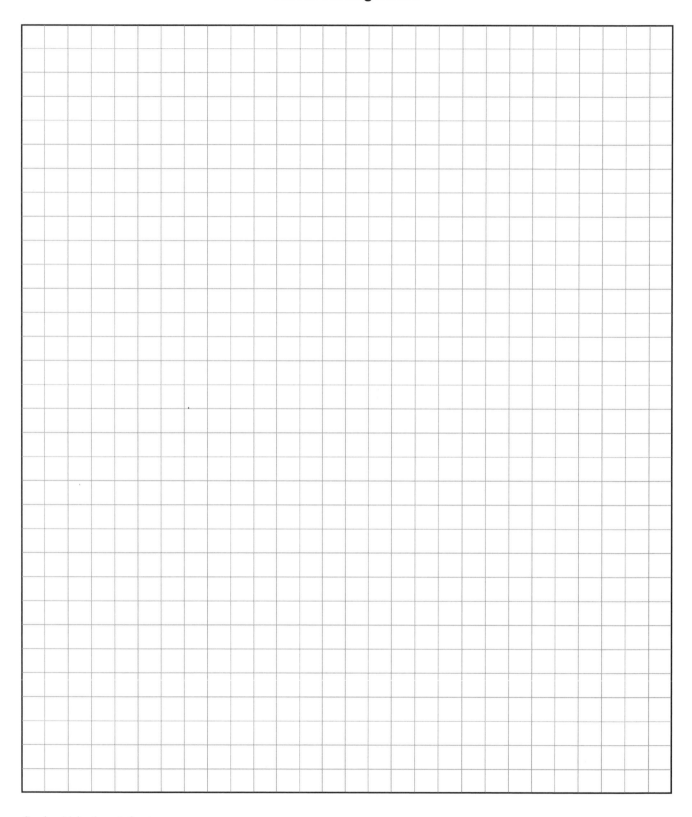

Scale: ¼ inch = 1 foot

(continued)

Name_____

■ To Review

1. Describe each of the areas listed below:
   Receiving area

   _____

   _____

   _____

   _____

   _____

   Playing area

   _____

   _____

   _____

   _____

   _____

   Napping area

   _____

   _____

   _____

   _____

   _____

   Diapering area

   _____

   _____

   _____

   _____

   _____

   Eating area

   _____

   _____

   _____

   _____

   _____

(continued)

Name_____

2. How could the space be improved?

_____

_____

_____

_____

_____

_____

_____

_____

Toy Inventory

Name _____

Date _____ Period _____

■ Objectives

After completing this activity, you will be able to

■ describe the environment of an infant-toddler program.

■ complete a toy inventory.

■ recommend additional equipment for the program.

■ Preparation

1. Make arrangements to visit an infant-toddler classroom.
2. Review the categories of toys in the chart below.

■ Setting

Place _____

Address _____

Telephone number _____

Contact person_____ Title _____

Date _____ Time _____ to _____

Number of children _____ Ages _____

Other information _____

_____

_____

■ To Do

Record toys available in the center under the appropriate categories in the chart. Then list additional toys for each category.

Category	Toys Present	Toys to Add
Looking toys		
Reaching and grasping toys		

(continued)

Name_____

Category	Toys Present	Toys to Add
Cuddling toys		
Squeezing and manipulative toys		
Kicking and hitting toys		
Pull and push toys		
Sound toys		
Large motor toys		
Small motor toys		

Evaluating Activity Areas for Toddlers

Activity C

Chapter 28

Name _____

Date _____ Period _____

■ Objectives

After completing this activity, you will be able to

- ■ evaluate the quality of the toddler activity areas.
- ■ recommend improvements in the toddler activity areas.

■ Preparation

1. Make arrangements to visit an infant-toddler program.
2. Review the questions below.

■ Setting

Place _____

Address _____

Telephone number _____

Contact person _____ Title _____

Date _____ Time _____ to _____

Number of children _____

Other information _____

_____

_____

■ To Do

As you observe the activity areas in the classroom, check *yes* or *no* under each category.

Evaluating Activity Area	Yes	No
Does the activity area encourage active exploration?		
Are the toys developmentally appropriate?		
Is there enough room for the children to play?		
Are there private places for the children to rest and observe?		
Are the materials at the children's eye level and within their reach?		
Are the heavy toys stored on the bottom shelves?		
Are the children provided choices so they can pursue their own interests?		
Are a variety of toys presented including those for solitary play and those that support cooperative play?		

(continued)

Evaluating Activity Area	Yes	No
Are the toys safe and checked frequently for sharp edges, loose pieces, and small parts that could be swallowed?		
Are toys rotated so the children are exposed to new toys from time to time?		
Are toys put away when not in use?		

■ To Review

1. What improvements could be made in this toddler activity area?

_____

_____

_____

_____

_____

_____

Programs for School-Age Children

Quality School-Age Programs

Activity A

Chapter 29

Name _____

Date _____ Period _____

■ Objectives

After completing this activity, you will be able to

■ evaluate the quality of a school-age child care program.

■ recommend improvement for the school-age program observed.

■ Preparation

1. Make arrangements to visit a school-age child care program.
2. Review the characteristics of a quality school-age program.

■ Setting

Place _____

Address _____

Telephone number _____

Contact person _____ Title _____

Date _____ Time _____ to _____

Number of children _____

Other information _____

_____

_____

■ To Do

As you observe the program, record evidence of how this program meets the characteristics of a quality school-age program.

Characteristics	Evidence
Low adult-child ratios	*(Example: There was one caregiver for every eight children.)*

(continued)

Name_____

Characteristics	Evidence
Warm, caring, well-trained staff	
Well-organized space with room for active play, quiet play, and interest centers	
Curriculum based on children's emerging interests and needs	
Parent involvement to achieve shared goals for children	
Flexible scheduling to allow for a balance of individual, small group, and large group activities	

■ To Review

1. Which characteristics of a quality school-age child care program were *not* observed? Explain.

_____

_____

_____

2. How would you rate the quality of this school-age program overall?

_____

_____

_____

(continued)

3. What area(s) could be improved, and what changes would you make?

_____

_____

_____

Scheduling School-Age Programs

Name _____

Date _____ **Period** _____

■ Objectives

After completing this activity, you will be able to

- ■ identify the parts of a school-age child care daily schedule.
- ■ evaluate a daily schedule.

■ Preparation

1. Arrange to visit a school-age child care program.
2. Before the observation, ask the director, principal, or teacher for a copy of the daily schedule and copy it in the space provided below.

■ Setting

Place _____

Address _____

Telephone number _____

Contact person _____ Title _____

Date _____ Time _____ to _____

Number of children _____

Other information _____

_____

_____

■ To Do

Write the daily schedule in the space provided. Evaluate the schedule by answering the questions that follow.

The Daily Schedule

(continued)

1. Does the teacher use arrival and departure times to share information with the children and parents? Explain.

    _____

    _____

    _____

2. Are there times for the children to self-select activities? Explain.

    _____

    _____

    _____

3. Are mealtimes used as a learning experience by providing the children with a sense of responsibility and community? Explain.

    _____

    _____

    _____

4. Is a rest time provided? Is it adequate to meet the children's needs? Explain.

    _____

    _____

    _____

5. Are there provisions for both indoor and outdoor activities? Explain.

    _____

    _____

    _____

6. Is there a balance between child-directed and teacher-directed activities? Explain.

    _____

    _____

    _____

7. Are children given responsibility for helping maintain the environment? Explain.

    _____

    _____

    _____

Guiding Children with Special Needs

Observing a Child with Special Needs

Activity A

Chapter 30

Name _____

Date _____ **Period** _____

■ Objectives

After completing this activity, you will be able to
- ■ describe the behavior of a child who has special needs in a classroom setting.
- ■ evaluate the assistance given to the child with special needs.

■ Preparation

1. Make arrangements to observe an early childhood program that has children with special needs.
2. Review the text information on children with special needs.

■ Setting

Place _____

Address _____

Telephone number _____

Contact person_____ Title _____

Date _____ Time _____ to _____

Number of children _____ Number of adults _____

Other information _____

_____

_____

■ To Do

Identify a child with special needs in the class. Then answer the following questions.

1. What is the nature of the child's special need?

_____

_____

_____

(continued)

2. Describe behaviors you observed that indicate the child may have a special need.

_____

_____

_____

3. Describe activities the child with special needs was able to do without assistance.

_____

_____

_____

4. Describe activities the child with special needs was unable to do without assistance.

_____

_____

_____

5. Describe the assistance the teacher gave the child.

_____

_____

_____

6. Describe any assistance other children gave the child.

_____

_____

_____

7. Did the child appear to be "labeled" by the teacher or other children? Explain your answer.

_____

_____

■ To Review

1. What evidence did you observe that would indicate that the needs of this child are or are not being met? Explain your answer.

_____

_____

_____

2. Describe any additional assistance the teacher might give this child.

_____

_____

_____

3. Describe any changes that could be made in the physical setting of the classroom that might help this child.

_____

_____

Parent Involvement

Volunteer Orientation

Activity A   **Name** _____

Chapter 31   **Date** _____ **Period** _____

■ Objective

After completing this activity, you will be able to

■ describe an orientation session for parent volunteers in an early childhood program.

■ Preparation

1. Make arrangements to attend an orientation session for parent volunteers.
2. Review the questions below.

■ Setting

Place _____

Address _____

Telephone number _____

Contact person_____ Title _____

Date _____ Time _____ to _____

Other information _____

_____

_____

■ To Do

As you observe the session, answer the questions below.

1. List the topics discussed during the orientation.

_____

_____

_____

_____

_____

_____

(continued)

Name_____

2. List the types of information shared by the teacher.

_____

_____

_____

_____

_____

_____

_____

_____

_____

_____

3. List four questions from parents and the teacher's responses.

A. Question:

Response:

B. Question:

Response:

C. Question:

Response:

D. Question:

Response:

Parent Involvement Purposes

Name _____

Date _____ **Period** _____

■ Objective

After completing this activity, you will be able to

■ describe the purposes and methods of parent involvement.

■ Preparation

1. Make arrangements to observe an early childhood program.
2. Review the objectives for parent involvement listed below.

■ Setting

Place _____

Address _____

Telephone number _____

Contact person_____ Title _____

Date _____Time _____ to _____

Number of children _____ Ages _____

Other information _____

_____

_____

■ To Do

Observe the program and ask the director or teacher how these objectives are met in their center. Record responses in the chart.

Parent Involvement Objectives	Center Activities Designed to Meet Objectives
Develop an understanding of child growth and development	
Gain confidence in their parenting roles	

(continued)

Name_____

Parent Involvement Objectives	Center Activities Designed to Meet Objectives
Learn about their children's experience in the center	
Understand their children by observing other children	
Learn new ways of positively interacting with children	
Become informed about community resources	
Foster the children's and parent's ability to interact with each other	
Extend learning from the center into the home	
Understand how a center-home partnership can promote the child's development	

A Career for You in Child Care

Interview Questions

Activity A

Chapter 32

Name _____

Date _____ Period _____

■ Objectives

After completing this activity, you will be able to

■ list qualifications needed for employment in a child care center.

■ list typical questions that might be asked during a job interview.

■ Preparation

Arrange to interview a director of a child care program.

■ Setting

Place _____

Address _____

Telephone number _____

Person interviewed _____ Title _____

Date _____ Time _____

■ To Do

Ask the director the following questions concerning what he or she looks for in a potential employee. Record the answers below.

1. What educational experience is required for the various positions at your center? _____

   _____

   _____

   _____

2. Is previous work experience necessary? _____

   _____

3. Do you require (and check) references? _____

   _____

(continued)

Name_____

4. What personal qualities do you look for in an employee? _____

_____

_____

_____

5. What other questions do you ask job applicants during an interview? _____

_____

_____

_____

_____

_____

_____

_____

6. Would you recommend a career in the child care field? Why or why not? _____

_____

_____

_____